Decluttering and Downsizing for Retirees

Simplify Your Life, Maximize Your Freedom

By Jeff Weidner
Boom Retirement Solutions

Published by Jeff Weidner
Wake Forest, NC

Limited Liability and Disclaimer of Warranty:
Every effort has been made by the author and publisher to ensure the accuracy and completeness of this book. However, the publisher and author make no representations or warranties of any kind, express or implied, about the accuracy or completeness of the contents. They specifically disclaim all implied warranties of merchantability or fitness for a particular purpose. The strategies and advice in this book may not be suitable for every situation. Neither the author nor the publisher shall be held liable for any loss of profit or other damages, including but not limited to special, incidental, consequential, or other damages arising out of the use or misuse of the information provided. Readers should consult with a qualified professional for personalized guidance.

First Edition
Published in Wake Forest, NC by Boom Retirement Solutions, 2025
Summary:
Decluttering and Downsizing for Retirees is a practical and supportive guide designed to help retirees simplify their lives by letting go of excess belongings and creating a home that reflects their current lifestyle. Blending step-by-step strategies with emotional insights, this book empowers readers to navigate the challenges of downsizing while embracing the freedom and opportunities that come with it.
Author: Jeff Weidner

Dedication

To all those approaching retirement, may you find the confidence and clarity to make the most of your retirement assets, reduce your taxes and create the retirement you deserve.
And to my family, whose support made this book possible.

Download your Free Book

https://books.jeffweidner.com/free

SCAN ME

DOWNLOAD FREE BOOK

Acknowledgments

Writing a book about *Decluttering and Downsizing for Retirees* that is both practical and heartfelt wouldn't have been possible without the support and insight of many wonderful people. I am deeply grateful to:

My clients, whose personal stories, questions, and experiences inspired much of the content in this book. Your courage in navigating life transitions and your willingness to share your journeys have been both a privilege and an inspiration.

The team at Boom Retirement Solutions, whose dedication to helping retirees simplify and secure their lives has been the foundation of this work. Your commitment to providing compassionate, thoughtful guidance makes our mission meaningful every day.

My mentors and colleagues, who have taught me the importance of meeting people where they are—whether that's in financial planning or life transitions like downsizing. Your wisdom and guidance helped shape the compassionate approach reflected in these pages.

The editorial team, whose attention to detail and thoughtful feedback ensured that this book is not only informative but also supportive and accessible. Your efforts have made this guide clearer and more helpful for readers at every stage of their downsizing journey.

My family, whose patience and encouragement during the writing process were invaluable. Your support kept me grounded and motivated, especially during the long days of writing and reflection.

And finally, **to you, the reader**—thank you for trusting this book to guide you through such a significant life transition. Your willingness to embrace change, simplify your life, and make space for what truly matters is inspiring. I hope this book offers both the practical tools and emotional support you need to navigate your downsizing journey with confidence and peace.

How to Use This Book

This book is your trusted companion on the journey to decluttering and downsizing, offering both practical advice and emotional support. Whether you're preparing for a move, simplifying your current living space, or helping a loved one through this process, you'll find tools and tips to guide you every step of the way.

Start Where You Are:

There's no right or wrong way to use this book. You can read it cover to cover or jump straight to the chapters that address your immediate needs. If you're unsure where to begin, start with the introduction and the first chapter, which help you explore your reasons for downsizing and prepare emotionally for the journey ahead.

Follow the Practical Guides:

Throughout the book, you'll find room-by-room guides, checklists, and decision-making tools designed to make the process manageable. These sections break down decluttering into bite-sized tasks, helping you stay organized and motivated without feeling overwhelmed.

Use the Worksheets and Templates:

In the appendices, you'll find customizable worksheets, from pre-downsizing assessments and room-by-room decluttering guides to moving timelines and financial planning tools. These resources are designed to help you stay on track and make informed decisions at every stage.

Embrace the Emotional Journey:

Downsizing isn't just about letting go of things—it's about navigating memories, family dynamics, and big life transitions. This book includes stories from people who have successfully downsized, as well as tips for managing the emotional side of the process. Refer back to these sections whenever you need reassurance or inspiration.

Keep It Flexible:

This book respects that everyone's journey is unique. Whether you're a minimalist at heart or sentimental about your belongings, the strategies here are flexible and adaptable to your needs. Take what works for you and leave the rest.

Refer Back Often:

Even after you've completed your downsizing, this book can serve as a resource for maintaining a clutter-free life and embracing new opportunities. Keep it handy for tips on staying organized and living intentionally in your simplified space.

Table of Contents

Introduction:

If you've ever opened a book about downsizing, only to find it feels more like an advertisement or a generic checklist, you're not alone. That was exactly the experience I had when I first started looking into this topic. What I needed was practical advice, yes—but I also needed emotional support, real stories, and guidance that didn't feel like it was trying to sell me something. That's why I decided to write this book. This isn't a sales pitch disguised as a guide. It's a friendly conversation about the real, sometimes complicated process of downsizing, with all the ups and downs that come with it.

Purpose of the Book: Addressing Real Concerns with Practical and Emotional Support

This book is designed to be your companion through the entire downsizing journey. We'll tackle everything from sorting through decades of belongings to navigating the emotional rollercoaster that often comes with letting go of sentimental items. But we won't just focus on the practicalities—because downsizing isn't just about "stuff." It's about memories, family dynamics, and envisioning the next exciting chapter of your life.

You won't find fluff here. What you will find are practical strategies that work, thoughtful tips to help you manage the stress, and a warm, understanding voice to remind you that you're not alone. Whether you're moving to a smaller home, transitioning to a retirement community, or simply decluttering to simplify your life, this book is here to help.

The Emotional and Practical Sides of Downsizing

Let's be honest: downsizing is rarely just about finding a smaller place to live. It's about confronting a lifetime of memories. Maybe it's the box of photos you haven't looked at in years but can't bear to throw away. Or the dining room table where you hosted countless family dinners. Even if you're excited about the next phase of life, saying goodbye to these things can be tough.

But there's also a practical side. Downsizing can free up your time, energy, and finances, giving you more freedom to enjoy your retirement. Less house to clean, fewer bills to pay, and more room (figuratively speaking) for the things that truly matter. This book is about finding that balance between honoring your past and embracing your future.

We'll explore how to sort through your belongings in a way that feels manageable, not overwhelming. You'll learn how to decide what to keep, what to donate, and what to let go of. And we'll talk about the financial side of things too—how to sell your home, avoid common pitfalls, and budget for your new lifestyle without feeling like you're sacrificing comfort or security.

Who This Book is For: Retirees, Empty Nesters, and Families Helping Loved Ones

This book is for anyone who's looking to simplify their life, but it's especially for retirees and empty nesters who are preparing for a new chapter. Maybe your kids have moved out, and you're left with a house that feels a little too big and a lot too quiet. Or perhaps you're thinking about moving closer to family or into a community where you can meet new people and try new things.

It's also for families helping loved ones through this process. If you're an adult child helping your parents downsize, you'll find tips here for navigating those sometimes tricky conversations and making the process as smooth and stress-free as possible.

Downsizing isn't a one-size-fits-all process. Everyone's journey is different, and this book respects that. Whether you're eager to embrace a minimalist lifestyle or you're feeling anxious about the idea of parting with your belongings, you'll find guidance here that meets you where you are.

Why This Book is Different

So, what makes this book different from the others? For starters, it's not trying to sell you anything. You won't find any hidden agendas or promotional pitches here. Instead, you'll find honest, practical advice that comes from real-life experience and a deep understanding of the challenges you might be facing.

Many downsizing books focus solely on the logistics—how to pack, what to sell, where to donate. That's important, of course, and we'll cover all of that. But what those books often miss is the emotional side of things. Downsizing isn't just a task to check off your to-do list. It's a major life transition, and it deserves to be treated with care and respect.

We'll talk about how to manage the stress and anxiety that can come with downsizing, how to honor your memories without feeling weighed down by them, and how to navigate family dynamics that might arise along the way. You'll find practical tips, yes—but you'll also find a supportive voice that understands what you're going through.

What to Expect in This Book

Throughout this book, you'll find a blend of practical advice and emotional support. We'll start by exploring why downsizing might be the right choice for you and how to prepare for the journey ahead. From there, we'll dive into the nitty-gritty details of sorting through your belongings, selling your home, and making the move to your new space.

But we won't stop there. Once you've made the move, we'll talk about how to adjust to your new home and embrace your new lifestyle. We'll also explore special situations, like moving into a retirement community or helping a loved one downsize. And we'll wrap up with tips for maintaining a simplified, clutter-free life and leaving a legacy that reflects what matters most to you. You'll find checklists and worksheets to help you stay organized, along with stories from people who've successfully navigated the downsizing process. These stories are here to inspire and reassure you, showing you that while downsizing can be challenging, it can also be incredibly rewarding.

Final Thoughts

Downsizing isn't just about letting go of things—it's about making space for what truly matters. It's about simplifying your life so you can focus on the people, experiences, and passions that bring you joy. Whether you're downsizing to save money, reduce stress, or embrace a new adventure, this book is here to guide you every step of the way.

This isn't just a guide—it's a conversation, and I'm glad you're here to join me. Let's dive in and start simplifying your life, one step at a time.

Chapter 1: The Why Behind Downsizing

Let's start with the big question: Why downsize?

It's a question I've asked myself more than once, and I'm guessing you have too. Maybe you've been mulling it over for months—or even years—but haven't quite taken the leap. Or maybe you're feeling a little overwhelmed by the idea of parting with your belongings, your home, or even a piece of your identity. That's completely normal.

Downsizing isn't just about moving to a smaller space; it's about making a conscious decision to simplify your life, to let go of what no longer serves you, and to make room for what truly matters.

But before we dive into the how of downsizing, let's take a moment to explore the why. Because understanding your reasons for downsizing can make all the difference in how you approach the process—and how you feel about it.

For many people, the decision to downsize comes from a desire for less stress and more freedom. Maybe your current home feels too big now that the kids have moved out, or maybe maintaining a large property is starting to feel more like a chore than a joy. Mowing a lawn, cleaning unused rooms, dealing with repairs—these things can start to feel like a burden when you'd rather be spending your time on things you love, like traveling, hobbies, or simply enjoying a slower pace of life.

Then there's the financial side of things. Downsizing can free up resources, allowing you to stretch your retirement savings further, reduce your monthly expenses, and maybe even put some extra cash toward experiences rather than things. Instead of sinking money into property taxes, utilities, and maintenance, you could use those funds for a long-awaited trip, a new hobby, or simply the peace of mind that comes with financial security.

Of course, there's also an emotional component to all of this. Your home is more than just four walls and a roof—it holds years, sometimes decades, of memories. The dining table where you gathered for family dinners, the bookshelf filled with novels you always meant to read, the closet with clothes from every stage of life. Letting go of a home, or even just the excess things in it, can feel like saying goodbye to a part of yourself. And that can be tough.

But here's the thing: Downsizing isn't about erasing the past. It's about curating your future. It's about keeping the things that truly bring you joy and letting go of the rest. Think of it as editing your life—keeping the best parts and clearing away the clutter so that you have more space (physically and mentally) to focus on what really matters.

I know that change can feel daunting. But imagine waking up in a home that feels just right—not too big, not too small, but exactly what you need. A place where every item has a purpose, where you're not weighed down by excess, where your space feels like a reflection of your present rather than a museum of the past. That's the real goal of downsizing: creating a home that fits your life today, not the life you had twenty years ago.

So, as we go through this journey together, I want you to keep one thing in mind: This isn't about giving things up. It's about gaining something even better. More freedom. More time. More peace of mind. And, most importantly, more room for the life you want to live now.

What excites you about downsizing? What worries you? Take a moment to reflect, because your reasons for downsizing will be your guiding light through this process. And trust me, once you get started, you might just find it's one of the best decisions you've ever made.

The Benefits of Downsizing: Financial Freedom, Simplified Living, and Less Stress

Let's talk about the perks first. Downsizing isn't just about saying goodbye to stuff; it's about saying hello to a life that's lighter, freer, and more focused on what brings you joy.

1. Financial Freedom

One of the most immediate benefits of downsizing is the financial relief it can bring. Let's face it: maintaining a large home can be expensive. Between property taxes, utility bills, and the never-ending list of repairs, the costs can add up quickly. By moving to a smaller space, you can significantly reduce these expenses, freeing up money for the things that truly matter—whether that's traveling, pursuing a hobby, or simply enjoying a more comfortable retirement.

I remember talking to a couple, Linda and Tom, who had lived in their four-bedroom home for over 30 years. Their kids had long since moved out, but they were still paying to heat and maintain rooms they barely used. When they finally decided to downsize to a two-bedroom condo, they were amazed at how much money they saved. "It's like getting a raise," Linda told me. "We're not just saving on bills; we're also not constantly fixing things. It's such a relief."

2. Simplified Living

There's something incredibly liberating about living with less. When you downsize, you're forced to evaluate what you really need—and what you don't. This process can be challenging, but it's also incredibly rewarding.

Think about it: how much time do you spend cleaning, organizing, or maintaining things you don't even use? Downsizing allows you to streamline your life, so you can spend less time managing your stuff and more time enjoying your life.

I'll never forget the story of my friend Margaret, who spent years holding onto a dining room set she inherited from her grandmother. It was beautiful, but it was also huge—and she rarely used it. When she finally decided to let it go, she was surprised by how freeing it felt. "I realized I was holding onto it out of guilt, not because I loved it," she said. "Now, I have a smaller table that actually fits my space, and I use it all the time. It's so much better."

3. Less Stress

Let's be honest: clutter can be stressful. It's not just the physical mess; it's the mental weight of knowing you have too much stuff and not enough space. Downsizing can help alleviate that stress by giving you a fresh start in a space that feels manageable and intentional.

I've heard so many people say that downsizing felt like a weight had been lifted off their shoulders. One woman, Carol, told me that after she downsized, she felt like she could breathe again. "I didn't realize how much my stuff was weighing me down until it was gone," she said. "Now, my home feels peaceful, and so do I."

Common Triggers for Downsizing: Retirement, Health Issues, and Empty Nesting

Now that we've covered the benefits of downsizing, let's dive into some of the most common reasons people decide to make the leap. These triggers often act as turning points, prompting us to take a step back, reassess our current living situation, and consider whether it still fits our needs and lifestyle.

---

1. Retirement

Retirement marks a significant shift in life—it's a time when many people finally get to enjoy the fruits of their labor. But with this newfound freedom comes a change in priorities and daily routines, and that often leads people to reconsider their living arrangements.

After decades of working, commuting, and juggling a busy household, you may find that the big house that once felt like the perfect family home now feels like more of a burden. Do you really need all those extra bedrooms if the kids have flown the nest? And honestly, who wants to spend their retirement mowing a massive lawn, cleaning unused rooms, or dealing with the constant upkeep of a large property?

For many retirees, downsizing is a chance to simplify life and focus on what truly matters. It's about creating a living space that supports the lifestyle you want in this new chapter—whether that's traveling the world, spending more time with grandkids, pursuing hobbies, or just enjoying some well-deserved relaxation. A smaller, more manageable home means less time spent on maintenance and more time spent doing what you love. Plus, the financial benefits—like lower utility bills, property taxes, and maintenance costs—can free up resources to fund your retirement dreams.

---

2. Health Issues

Our health plays a huge role in determining where and how we live, and as we age, it's common to face challenges that make maintaining a larger home more difficult. Mobility issues, chronic illnesses, or even just the natural wear and tear of aging can turn simple tasks—like climbing stairs, cleaning multiple rooms, or navigating a sprawling yard—into daily hurdles.

Downsizing to a more accessible living space can be a game-changer. Single-level homes, condos, or retirement communities often come equipped with features designed to make life easier and safer—think wider doorways, walk-in showers, and minimal steps. These changes might seem small, but they can have a big impact on your quality of life.

I remember chatting with a man named Robert, who had lived in a charming two-story house for decades. After a knee replacement surgery, he found that the stairs he used to breeze up and down had become a real challenge. "At first, I didn't want to admit I needed to move," he told me. "It felt like giving up." But after relocating to a single-story condo, Robert discovered a new sense of freedom. "I didn't realize how much the stairs were holding me back until I didn't have to deal with them anymore. Life just feels easier now."

For many, downsizing isn't just about simplifying—it's about reclaiming independence and ensuring that your home is a place of comfort, not stress.

---

3. Empty Nesting

There's a unique mix of emotions that comes when your children move out—pride, nostalgia, and maybe even a little sadness. But as the dust settles, many empty nesters find themselves staring at a house that suddenly feels much too big, filled with rooms that sit untouched and clutter that's accumulated over the years.

Empty nesting can be bittersweet, but it's also an opportunity to rethink how you want to live moving forward. Do you really need the formal dining room that only got used on holidays? Or the multiple guest bedrooms that now collect dust? Downsizing allows you to let go of the excess space—and the excess stuff—that no longer serves you.

For many, this transition is about more than just square footage; it's about redefining your home to reflect who you are now, not who you were when the kids were growing up. It's a chance to create a space that feels cozy, efficient, and perfectly suited to your current lifestyle. Maybe it's a chic downtown condo close to your favorite restaurants and cultural spots, or perhaps it's a smaller home with a beautiful garden where you can finally indulge your green thumb.

And let's not forget the emotional weight that comes with holding onto a home that feels like a shrine to the past. Downsizing can be a liberating process—one that helps you let go of what was and embrace what's next.

In the end, whether it's retirement, health challenges, or an empty nest, these life changes serve as reminders that our homes should evolve with us. Downsizing isn't about giving up—it's about gaining the freedom to live the life you want, in a space that fits who you are today.

Recognizing When It's Time to Downsize

So, how do you really know when it's time to downsize? The truth is, there's no universal rule or perfect timing that applies to everyone. Downsizing is a deeply personal decision that depends on your lifestyle, needs, and goals. However, there are some common signs that might suggest it's time to reevaluate your living situation and consider making a change.

Let's explore a few of these key indicators:

1. You're Feeling Overwhelmed

If the thought of cleaning, organizing, or maintaining your home leaves you feeling stressed or exhausted, it could be a sign that your current space is simply too large or too demanding. Maybe you've noticed that the weekend is spent more on household chores than on activities you actually enjoy. Or perhaps you've started to put off basic tasks—like yard work, repairs, or even deep cleaning—because they feel like too much to handle. Over time, the responsibilities that come with a bigger home can become a heavy burden, especially as life changes. What once felt like a manageable routine may now feel like an endless to-do list. Downsizing can help lighten that load, giving you more time and energy to focus on the things that truly matter to you—whether that's traveling, spending time with loved ones, or simply enjoying a slower pace of life.

2. You're Not Using All Your Space

Take a walk through your home with fresh eyes. Are there rooms that sit untouched for weeks—or even months—at a time? Maybe there's a guest bedroom that only gets used during the holidays or a formal dining room that's gathering dust. Closets may be packed with items you haven't thought about in years, and storage areas might be overflowing with things you no longer need.

If you find yourself living in just a small section of your home while the rest goes unused, it might be time to reconsider whether you really need all that space. After all, why pay for (and maintain) square footage that doesn't serve a purpose in your daily life? Downsizing can help you streamline your living environment, eliminating unnecessary rooms and focusing on a space that fits your current lifestyle. It's not about losing space—it's about gaining efficiency and comfort.

---

3. You're Ready for a Change

Sometimes, the desire to downsize doesn't come from necessity—it comes from a sense of excitement or curiosity about the future. You might feel a pull toward simplifying your life, exploring new places, or embracing a different way of living. Maybe you've always dreamed of moving to a vibrant city, a cozy coastal town, or even a retirement community with built-in social activities. Downsizing can be a fresh start—a chance to reinvent your daily routine and design a lifestyle that reflects where you are now, not where you were ten or twenty years ago. It's about embracing new opportunities and shedding the parts of your life (and your home) that no longer bring you joy. This kind of change can be invigorating, offering a sense of freedom and possibility that's hard to achieve when you're tied to a larger, more demanding home.

Other Signs It Might Be Time to Downsize:

- **Financial Considerations:** If your housing costs are starting to feel like a strain on your budget, downsizing can free up money for other priorities, like travel, hobbies, or retirement savings. Lower utility bills, reduced property taxes, and fewer maintenance expenses can make a big difference.

- **Mobility or Accessibility Challenges:** If health issues or mobility concerns are making it difficult to navigate your home—think steep stairs, narrow hallways, or hard-to-reach storage—it might be time to consider a more accessible living space.

- **Life Changes:** Major life events, like retirement, the loss of a spouse, or children moving out, can leave you reevaluating whether your current home still meets your needs.

Final Thoughts

Downsizing is a deeply personal decision, and there's no right or wrong time to do it. What matters is that you're making a choice that feels right for you—one that aligns with your values, your goals, and your vision for the future.

In the next chapter, we'll dive into the practical side of downsizing, exploring how to create a plan that works for you. But for now, take a moment to reflect on your reasons for downsizing. What are you hoping to gain? What are you ready to let go of?

Remember, downsizing isn't just about saying goodbye to stuff; it's about saying hello to a life that's simpler, freer, and more focused on what truly matters.

Chapter 2: The Emotional Impact of Downsizing

Downsizing isn't just about sorting through your belongings or finding a smaller place to live. It's about confronting a lifetime of memories, emotions, and relationships—all of which can make the process feel overwhelming at times.

I'll admit, when I first started downsizing, I thought it would be a straightforward task. I'd make a few piles—keep, donate, toss—and be done with it. But as I began sorting through my things, I realized that every item seemed to carry a story, a memory, or a piece of my identity. That's when it hit me: downsizing isn't just about letting go of stuff; it's about letting go of the past.

And that's what we're going to talk about in this chapter: the emotional side of downsizing. Because while it's important to have a plan and stay organized, it's equally important to acknowledge and honor the feelings that come up along the way.

Facing Sentimental Attachments

Every photo album, piece of furniture, or trinket tucked away in a drawer has a story to tell. Maybe it's the rocking chair where you held your grandchild for the first time, or the stack of letters from a loved one who's no longer here. These aren't just objects—they're tangible links to moments and people who shaped your life.

When you start to part with these items, it can feel like you're erasing a part of your history. That's a heavy feeling, and it's perfectly normal. The key is to recognize that your memories don't reside in the objects themselves but in your heart and mind. Taking photos of cherished items before letting them go, or writing down the stories attached to them, can help preserve those memories without holding onto the physical clutter.

Guilt and Obligation

Another emotional hurdle is the guilt that can come with downsizing. Maybe you're holding onto a gift from someone special, even though it doesn't serve a purpose in your life anymore. Or perhaps you feel obligated to keep family heirlooms, even if they don't fit in your new space.

It's important to remember that keeping an item out of guilt doesn't honor the person who gave it to you. Their love and thoughtfulness aren't tied to that object. If you're struggling to let go, consider passing the item on to someone who will appreciate it, or donating it to a cause that matters to you. This way, the item continues to bring joy and purpose beyond your home.

Identity and Change

Downsizing can also stir up questions about your identity. You might wonder, "Who am I without all these things?" or "What does it mean to live in a smaller space?" It's a shift, no doubt, and it can feel unsettling at first.

But here's the thing: you are not defined by your possessions. Letting go of excess stuff can actually be liberating, giving you the freedom to focus on what truly matters—your relationships, experiences, and passions. Downsizing is an opportunity to redefine what's important to you and to create a living space that reflects the person you are today, not just who you were in the past.

Coping with the Emotional Rollercoaster

It's okay to feel a mix of emotions as you downsize—sadness, relief, anxiety, even excitement. The process can be a rollercoaster, but acknowledging your feelings instead of pushing them aside makes it easier to navigate. Give yourself permission to take breaks when needed. Talk to friends or family members about what you're feeling. Sometimes just sharing your thoughts out loud can lighten the emotional load. And remember, it's perfectly fine to keep a few sentimental items that truly bring you joy. Downsizing doesn't mean stripping your life of everything you love—it's about making thoughtful choices that support your next chapter.

Embracing the New Chapter

While downsizing involves letting go, it's also about embracing new possibilities. A smaller space can mean less maintenance and more time for the things you enjoy. It can bring financial freedom, reduce stress, and even improve your overall well-being.

Think of downsizing not as losing, but as gaining—gaining clarity, simplicity, and the opportunity to live more intentionally. You're creating a home that supports your current lifestyle and future goals, and that's something to be proud of.

In the next chapter, we'll dive into practical tips and strategies to make the downsizing process smoother. But for now, take a moment to reflect on the emotional journey. It's a significant part of the process, and honoring it will make the transition not just easier, but more meaningful.

Understanding the Emotional Weight of "Stuff"

Let's start with the elephant in the room: why is it so hard to let go of things?

For many of us, our belongings are more than just objects; they're symbols of who we are, where we've been, and what we've accomplished. That old sweater in the back of your closet? It might remind you of a trip you took with your spouse. The box of childhood toys in the attic? It could bring back memories of your kids when they were little.

The problem is, when we hold onto things for sentimental reasons, they can start to weigh us down—both physically and emotionally. I remember talking to a woman named Susan, who had been holding onto her late husband's clothes for years. "I knew I needed to let them go," she told me, "but every time I tried, I felt like I was losing a part of him all over again."

The truth is, letting go of stuff can feel like letting go of a piece of yourself. But here's the thing: your memories aren't stored in your belongings. They're stored in your heart. And while it's okay to keep a few special items, holding onto everything can prevent you from moving forward.

doesn't mean stripping your life of everything you love—it's about making thoughtful choices that support your next chapter.

Practical Steps to Let Go

So, how do you start to let go?

One approach is to ask yourself a few key questions:

• Does this item bring me joy or serve a purpose in my life today?
• If I were to move tomorrow, would I take this with me?
• Am I holding onto this out of love, or out of guilt or obligation?
These questions can help you separate the things that truly matter from the things that are just taking up space. And remember, it's okay to take your time. Downsizing is a process, not a race.

Coping with Sentimental Attachments and Family Heirlooms

Now, let's talk about one of the trickiest parts of downsizing: dealing with sentimental items and family heirlooms. It's not just about stuff—it's about memories, relationships, and pieces of our past that feel woven into who we are.

I'll be honest: this is where I struggled the most. My grandmother's delicate china set, my dad's old, worn toolbox, my kids' colorful artwork from kindergarten—how could I possibly let go of these things? Each item felt like a little time capsule, carrying moments I wasn't ready to part with.

But here's the truth I discovered along the way: you don't have to let go of *everything*. Downsizing isn't about erasing your past; it's about being intentional with what you choose to carry forward. It's making room for the life you want to live now while honoring the memories that shaped you.

If you're feeling stuck, here are a few strategies that helped me navigate this emotional terrain. Hopefully, they'll make your journey a little easier too.

1. Choose a Few Meaningful Items

Instead of keeping everything, focus on selecting a few items that hold the most meaning for you. Think about what truly brings you joy or evokes strong, positive memories.

For instance, instead of holding onto the entire set of your grandmother's china that rarely sees the light of day, maybe you keep just one beautiful teacup and saucer. You can display them somewhere special, where you'll see them often and smile. Or, instead of keeping every single piece of your kids' artwork—which, let's face it, can pile up fast—choose a few standout pieces that capture their creativity and spirit.

This approach helps you keep the memories alive without overwhelming your space.

2. Take Photos

Sometimes, it's not the item itself but the memory it holds that's hard to part with. If you're struggling to let go of something, consider taking a photo of it before you say goodbye.

I did this with my dad's old toolbox. I took a few pictures of it, especially focusing on the little nicks and scratches that told stories of countless projects we tackled together. Now, those photos sit in an album, and whenever I flip through, I'm reminded of those special moments. The toolbox found a new home, but the memories stayed with me.

This method works wonderfully for bulky or impractical items you don't have space for but still want to remember.

3. Pass It On

If you have family heirlooms or sentimental items you no longer need but can't bear to simply discard, think about who in your life might appreciate them.

Passing these treasures on to someone else can be a beautiful way to honor their significance. For example, you might gift your grandmother's china to a niece or nephew who's just starting their own family. Not only does this keep the item in the family, but it also allows it to create new memories in someone else's life.

I remember talking to a man named John, who had inherited a collection of antique tools from his father. He didn't have any practical use for them, but he couldn't bear the thought of tossing them out or letting them gather dust in his garage. After some thought, he decided to donate the tools to a local museum that showcased historical artifacts from the community. "It felt good to know they'd be appreciated," he told me. "And it was a way to honor my dad's memory without holding onto something I didn't need."

Sometimes, letting go isn't about losing something—it's about giving it new life.

At the end of the day, downsizing sentimental items is less about the physical objects and more about how you hold onto the memories. It's okay to feel emotional; it's a sign that those moments mattered. But by being thoughtful about what you keep and how you let go, you can create a living space that honors your past *and* supports your future.

Remember, your memories aren't tied to things—they're tied to your heart. And that's something you'll carry with you wherever you go.

Managing Stress and Anxiety During the Process

Let's face it: downsizing isn't just about moving to a smaller space—it's about navigating a sea of emotions, memories, and decisions. There's the physical labor of sorting through decades' worth of belongings, the emotional tug-of-war that comes with letting go of sentimental items, and the logistical puzzle of coordinating a move. It's no wonder that many people feel completely overwhelmed by the process.

But here's the silver lining: with the right approach and mindset, you *can* manage the stress and make this journey feel less daunting. It might even become an opportunity for reflection and growth.

1. Take It One Step at a Time

One of the biggest pitfalls people encounter is trying to tackle everything at once. Standing in the middle of a room filled with boxes and clutter, it's easy to feel like the task is insurmountable. But here's the trick: break the process down into bite-sized, manageable chunks.

Start small. Maybe it's just one drawer, one closet, or one bookshelf. Celebrate those little wins. Each small task you complete adds up, creating a momentum that makes the next step easier. It's like climbing a mountain—you don't reach the top in one leap, but step by step, you'll get there.

Take Karen's story, for example. She was a widow in her late 60s, staring at a house full of memories and feeling completely paralyzed. "I didn't even know where to start," she told me. But one day, she picked up a small box from her kitchen junk drawer and began sorting. That simple action sparked a chain reaction. "I felt like I was finally making progress, even if it was just a little bit at a time," she said. By focusing on small, manageable tasks, Karen transformed what felt like an impossible job into a series of achievable goals.

2. Ask for Help

Here's something many people forget: **you don't have to do this alone**. Whether it's calling on family, friends, or professionals, asking for help can ease the physical and emotional burden.

Consider enlisting a professional organizer—they're not just for the rich and famous! These experts can help you make objective decisions, especially when emotions run high. But if hiring someone isn't your style, lean on your support system. Invite a friend over to help sort through old clothes or ask your kids to spend a weekend packing. And don't underestimate the power of simply *talking* to someone about how you're feeling. Downsizing can stir up unexpected emotions—grief, anxiety, even guilt. Sharing those feelings with a trusted friend or counselor can lighten the emotional load and remind you that you're not alone in this.

3. Practice Self-Care

Let's be honest: downsizing isn't just a physical task—it's an emotional marathon. That's why self-care isn't a luxury during this time—it's a necessity.

Make time for activities that replenish your energy and bring you joy. Maybe that's taking a daily walk in the fresh air, curling up with a favorite book, or simply sitting quietly with a cup of tea. And don't forget to nourish your body with healthy meals and get enough rest. You'll be surprised at how much better you'll feel when you take care of yourself along the way.

It's also okay to step back when things feel too heavy. Give yourself permission to pause, reflect, and even take a day off from the process. You're not on a deadline (unless you've sold your house already—then maybe a *little* hustle is needed!).

Navigating Family Dynamics: Conversations with Adult Children

Now, let's talk about one of the trickiest parts of downsizing—**family dynamics**. If you have adult children, chances are they have opinions. Lots of them. Maybe they think you should keep that old dining table for "family gatherings" or insist you hold onto every childhood drawing they ever made. And while their intentions are usually good, these conversations can sometimes feel overwhelming, or even frustrating.

So, how do you navigate these discussions without losing your cool or feeling pressured?

1. Set Clear Boundaries

First things first: remember that **this is your journey**. While it's perfectly fine to ask for input, the final decision rests with you. You've spent a lifetime building your home and collecting your treasures—it's up to you to decide what stays and what goes.

It's helpful to be upfront with your children from the start. Let them know you appreciate their thoughts, but ultimately, you're making decisions based on what feels right for *you*. Setting this boundary early can prevent misunderstandings and emotional tug-of-wars later.

2. Be Honest About Your Feelings

Downsizing isn't just about physical belongings—it's about navigating emotions, both yours and your family's. If you're feeling overwhelmed, anxious, or even a little sad, **say so**. Let your kids know that this is a big transition for you and that their support, not judgment, is what you need most.

Sometimes, simply sharing how you feel can open the door to more compassionate and understanding conversations. It helps your family see things from your perspective and fosters a supportive environment rather than a confrontational one.

3. Involve Them in the Process

If your kids are willing, invite them to be part of the process. Not only does this give them a sense of involvement, but it can also help ease the emotional burden for everyone.

For instance, you might ask them to help sort through old family photos or decide what to do with heirlooms. This can turn a potentially stressful task into a cherished opportunity to reminisce and connect. Plus, it helps clarify what items they truly care about—and which ones they might just be holding onto out of habit.

Take Linda's story, for example. She was struggling because her kids kept insisting she keep things she no longer wanted. "It was so frustrating," she said. "But then I sat them down and explained that I needed to do this for myself. Once they understood how I was feeling, they were much more supportive." By involving them in an honest conversation, Linda was able to find a balance between honoring her family's feelings and staying true to her own needs.

Final Thoughts

Downsizing is more than just a task—it's a journey. And like any journey, it comes with its fair share of twists and turns. There will be moments when you feel a wave of relief as you clear out a space that's been cluttered for years. But there will also be moments when you stumble upon an old photo, a keepsake, or a piece of furniture that holds a lifetime of memories, and suddenly, the process feels a lot heavier.

It's perfectly normal to feel a mix of emotions—joy, sadness, even frustration. Let yourself feel them. Downsizing isn't just about sorting through belongings; it's about processing the memories attached to them. It's about acknowledging the life you've built so far and deciding what parts of that life you want to carry with you into this next chapter. And through every step of this journey, remember: you're not alone. Many have walked this path before you, and many are walking it alongside you now.

In the next chapter, we'll shift gears and dive into the practical side of downsizing. We'll explore how to create a plan that fits your unique needs, how to stay organized, and how to make thoughtful decisions about what to keep and what to let go. But before we get there, take a moment to pause. Reflect on the emotional side of this process. What feelings are bubbling to the surface? Are there specific items or memories you're finding it hard to part with? And perhaps even more importantly, what are you feeling ready to let go of—not just physically, but emotionally too?

Because here's the thing: downsizing isn't just about saying goodbye to "stuff." It's about creating space—for new experiences, for freedom, for a life that feels lighter and more focused on what truly matters to you. It's about opening the door to a simpler, more intentional way of living.

We've only just begun this journey together, and there's so much more to explore. But for now, take comfort in knowing that every step you take, no matter how small, is moving you closer to a life that feels more aligned with who you are and where you want to go.

Chapter 3: Planning Your Downsizing Journey

Let's talk about planning. I know, I know—planning might not sound like the most exciting topic, but trust me, it's the secret sauce to making downsizing feel manageable instead of overwhelming. Think of it like this: if downsizing is a journey (and it is), then planning is your roadmap. Without it, you might end up going in circles, feeling lost, or worse—giving up altogether.

But here's the good news: planning doesn't have to be complicated. In fact, it can be as simple as sitting down with a cup of coffee, a notebook, and a willingness to dream a little about what you want your life to look like on the other side of this process. Imagine waking up in a home that feels just right—not too big, not too cluttered, but cozy and filled with the things that truly matter to you. That's the goal we're working toward.

In this chapter, we're going to break it all down: how to create a personalized downsizing plan, how to set realistic timelines, and how to identify your goals so you can move forward with confidence. You don't need to have it all figured out today, but by the end of this chapter, you'll have a clear, actionable path to follow.

Why Planning Matters

You might be wondering, "Do I really need a plan? Can't I just start sorting through my stuff?" Sure, you *could* dive right in, but without a plan, you might find yourself overwhelmed by decisions, stuck on sentimental items, or running out of steam halfway through. Planning helps you stay organized, focused, and motivated. It gives you a sense of direction and progress, even when the process feels tough.

Step 1: Visualize Your Ideal Future

Before you start packing boxes or deciding what to keep, take a moment to picture your future. What does your ideal downsized life look like? Are you in a smaller house, a cozy condo, or maybe even traveling the world with fewer possessions to tie you down? Think about how you want to spend your days, what activities bring you joy, and what kind of space supports that lifestyle.

Write down your vision. This isn't just a fun exercise—it's a crucial part of staying motivated. When the going gets tough (and it might), you'll have a clear reminder of why you're doing this.

Step 2: Set Your Goals

Once you have a vision, it's time to set some goals. These can be big or small, but they should be specific and meaningful to you. Maybe you want to reduce your belongings by 50%, move into a one-story home, or create a more organized living space that's easier to maintain. Whatever your goals are, write them down and keep them visible as you go through the process.

Step 3: Create a Timeline

Downsizing doesn't have to happen overnight. In fact, it's better if it doesn't. Give yourself plenty of time to sort through your belongings, make decisions, and adjust to the changes. Break the process into smaller, manageable steps with realistic deadlines. For example, you might spend a week tackling one room at a time or set a goal to have everything sorted within three months.

Step 4: Make a Checklist

A checklist is your best friend during the downsizing journey. It keeps you organized and gives you a sense of accomplishment as you tick off each task. Start by listing all the areas of your home that need attention—closets, kitchen, garage, etc.—and then break those down into smaller tasks, like "Sort through winter clothes" or "Donate old kitchen gadgets."

Step 5: Stay Flexible

Even the best-laid plans can hit a few bumps along the way. Life happens, and you might need to adjust your timeline or goals as you go. That's okay! The important thing is to stay flexible and keep moving forward. Remember, this is your journey, and there's no one right way to do it.

Creating a Personalized Downsizing Plan

The first step in any successful downsizing journey is creating a plan that works for you. Not your neighbor, not your best friend, and definitely not your adult children—*you*. Because here's the thing: downsizing isn't a one-size-fits-all process. What works for someone else might not work for you, and that's perfectly okay. Your life, your memories, and your needs are unique. So, let's make sure your downsizing plan reflects that.

1. Assess Your Current Situation

Before you can figure out where you're going, you need to know where you are. This step is all about taking a good, honest look at your current living situation.

- **How much space do you have?** Walk through your home with fresh eyes. Are there rooms you rarely enter? Spaces that feel more like storage units than living areas?

- **How much of it are you actually using?** It's common to have rooms that go untouched for months. Maybe that formal dining room only gets used twice a year, or the guest bedroom has become a catch-all for old holiday decorations.

- **How do you feel about your home?** This is perhaps the most important question. Is your home a source of comfort and joy, or does it feel like a burden?

I remember talking to a woman named Carol, who had lived in her four-bedroom house for over 30 years. It was the house where she raised her kids, hosted countless family gatherings, and celebrated life's milestones. But when I asked her how she felt about her home now, she paused and said, "It's not my home anymore. It's just a house full of stuff." That moment was a turning point for her. It helped her realize she was ready for a change—not because she didn't cherish her memories, but because she wanted to create new ones in a space that fit her current life.

2. Define Your Vision

Once you've assessed your current situation, it's time to dream a little. What do you want your life to look like after you downsize? This is your opportunity to reimagine your future and create a lifestyle that brings you joy and peace.

- **Do you want a smaller home with less maintenance?** Maybe a cozy condo with a beautiful view sounds appealing.

- **Are you dreaming of a retirement community?** Somewhere you can meet new people, join clubs, and stay active.

- **Are you considering moving in with family?** To be closer to your grandkids and share more day-to-day moments.

Whatever your vision, *write it down.* Be as specific as possible. For example, instead of saying, "I want a smaller home," you might say, "I want a two-bedroom condo with a balcony where I can sit and drink my morning coffee." The more detailed your vision, the easier it will be to make decisions along the way.

3. Break It Down into Steps

Now that you have a vision, it's time to break it down into actionable steps. Downsizing can feel overwhelming if you look at it as one giant task. But when you break it into smaller, manageable pieces, it becomes much more doable.

- **Make a list of everything that needs to happen before you can move.** This might include decluttering, selling your home, finding a new place to live, and packing.

- **Prioritize the tasks.** What needs to happen first? For example, you can't sell your home until it's decluttered and staged.
- **Delegate or ask for help.** Don't be afraid to reach out to friends, family, or even professional organizers. Downsizing doesn't have to be a solo journey.

Setting Realistic Timelines: 6-Month, 3-Month, and Last-Minute Moves

One of the most common questions I hear is, "How long does downsizing take?" The answer, of course, depends on your situation. But in general, it's a good idea to give yourself plenty of time—especially if you're dealing with a lifetime of belongings. Rushing can add unnecessary stress and lead to decisions you might regret later.
Let's take a closer look at three common timelines: 6-month, 3-month, and last-minute moves.

1. The 6-Month Plan

If you have six months to downsize, you're in a great position. This timeline gives you plenty of time to declutter, sell your home, and find a new place to live without feeling rushed.

Sample Timeline for a 6-Month Plan:

- **Months 1-2:** Start decluttering. Focus on one room at a time. Don't be afraid to ask for help from family or friends. This is also a great time to reflect on what items truly add value to your life.
- **Months 3-4:** List your home for sale (if applicable) and start looking for a new place to live. Take your time to find a space that aligns with the vision you created.

- **Months 5-6:** Pack, move, and settle into your new home. Since you've given yourself plenty of time, you can unpack at a comfortable pace and make your new space feel like home.

I remember talking to a couple, Jim and Linda, who followed a 6-month plan when they downsized. "It felt like we had all the time in the world," Linda told me. "We were able to take our time and really think about what we wanted to keep and what we could let go of. It made the process almost enjoyable."

2. The 3-Month Plan

If you have three months to downsize, you'll need to move a little faster—but it's still completely doable. The key is to stay organized and focused.

Sample Timeline for a 3-Month Plan:

- **Month 1:** Declutter and organize. Focus on the areas that will take the most time, like the attic, basement, or garage. These spaces often hold the most 'just in case' items that are hardest to part with.

- **Month 2:** List your home for sale (if applicable) and start looking for a new place to live. You might need to make quicker decisions, but trust your instincts.

- **Month 3:** Pack, move, and settle into your new home. You might need to be more efficient with packing—consider labeling boxes clearly and keeping an inventory to stay organized.

One thing to keep in mind with a 3-month plan is that you might need to make some decisions more quickly than you'd like. For example, you might not have time to sell everything you don't want, so you might need to donate or give away some items.

3. The Last-Minute Move

Sometimes, life throws us curveballs, and we don't have the luxury of time. Whether it's an unexpected health issue, a sudden change in family dynamics, or an opportunity that's too good to pass up, last-minute moves happen. And while they can be stressful, they're not impossible.

Sample Timeline for a Last-Minute Move:

- **Week 1:** Focus on the essentials. Pack the things you know you'll need in your new home, like clothes, toiletries, medications, and important documents. Think about what you'd take if you were going on an extended trip—those are your essentials.

- **Week 2:** Declutter as much as possible. If you don't have time to sort through everything, consider hiring a professional organizer or asking friends and family for help. You can always deal with non-essential items later.

- **Week 3:** Move and settle into your new home. Give yourself grace during this process. It might not be perfect, but you're making progress.

I'll never forget the story of a woman named Margaret, who had to downsize in just three weeks after her husband passed away. "It was overwhelming," she told me. "But I focused on the things that mattered most, and I asked for help when I needed it. In the end, it all worked out."

Identifying Your Goals: Moving to a Smaller Home, Assisted Living, or with Family

Finally, let's talk about goals. Because downsizing isn't just about getting rid of stuff; it's about creating a life that feels right for you. And to do that, you need to know what you're working toward.

1. Moving to a Smaller Home

If your goal is to move to a smaller home, the key is to focus on what you *really* need.

- **Think about your daily routine.** What spaces do you use the most? If you love to cook, prioritize a kitchen with plenty of counter space. But if you rarely entertain, you might be able to downsize your dining room.

- **Consider storage solutions.** Even in a smaller home, there are creative ways to store the things you love. Look for furniture that doubles as storage or consider off-site storage for seasonal items.

2. Moving to Assisted Living

If you're considering assisted living, the process might look a little different.

- **Think about what items will fit in your new space.** Most assisted living apartments are smaller, so you'll need to prioritize the essentials. A comfortable chair, some favorite photos, and a few cherished keepsakes can make the space feel like home.

- **Consider what you'll need to maintain your independence.** This might include adaptive tools, easy-to-reach storage solutions, or familiar items that bring you comfort.

3. Moving in with Family

If your goal is to move in with family, communication is key.

- **Talk about expectations.** Sit down with your loved ones and discuss what you'll need to bring and what you'll need to leave behind.
- **Create a space that feels like yours.** Even if you're moving into a spare bedroom, bring a few pieces of furniture or decorations that make the space feel like home.

For example, you might want to bring your favorite reading chair or a special quilt, but you might not need to bring your entire collection of books or knickknacks.

Final Thoughts

Planning your downsizing journey might feel overwhelming at first, but it doesn't have to be. Think of it as an adventure—a chance to reshape your life, make room for new experiences, and focus on what truly matters. By breaking the process down into manageable steps, setting realistic timelines, and identifying your personal goals, you can create a plan that's not only doable but also meaningful. This isn't just about moving from a bigger space to a smaller one; it's about crafting a lifestyle that reflects your values, needs, and dreams.

Consider the progress you've made so far. You've thought about why you want to downsize, identified the benefits it can bring, and started to outline a roadmap to guide your journey. That's no small feat! Taking those first steps can be the hardest part, but you've done it—and that's something to be proud of.

As you continue, remember to give yourself grace. Downsizing isn't a race; it's a process. You might hit some bumps along the way, and that's okay. The key is to stay flexible and open-minded. Adjust your plan if needed, and keep your eyes on the bigger picture. After all, this journey is about more than just letting go of things—it's about embracing a future that feels lighter, freer, and more in tune with the life you want to live.

In the next chapter, we'll dive into the nitty-gritty of decluttering. This is where the real fun begins! We'll explore practical strategies for sorting through your belongings, deciding what to keep, what to donate, and what to let go of. Whether you're dealing with a lifetime of memories or just trying to clear out a few overstuffed closets, we'll guide you through the process with tips, tricks, and a few heartfelt stories to keep you inspired.

But for now, take a moment to reflect. What's your vision for the future? What does your ideal living space look and feel like? And what small steps can you take today to move closer to that vision? Maybe it's as simple as making a list, setting a date to tackle a specific room, or even just picturing how good it will feel to have a home that truly serves your needs.

Remember, downsizing isn't just about letting go of stuff; it's about making space for what truly matters. It's about creating a home that reflects who you are now and supports the life you want to lead moving forward.

Are you ready to roll up your sleeves and get started? In this next chapter, Chapter 4: Decluttering Made Simple, we'll simplify the decluttering process, breaking it down into easy, actionable steps. You'll learn how to tackle each room with confidence, make decisions without second-guessing yourself, and even find joy in the process of letting go. We'll cover everything from sentimental items to everyday clutter, and by the end, you'll feel empowered to create a space that's not only organized but also filled with meaning and purpose.
Let's dive in!

Chapter 4: Decluttering Made Simple

Let's talk about decluttering. I know, I know—it's one of those words that can make even the most organized person break out in a cold sweat. But here's the thing: decluttering doesn't have to be overwhelming. In fact, when done right, it can feel like a breath of fresh air.
Think of it this way: decluttering is like peeling an onion. You start with the outer layers—the easy stuff—and work your way inward, tackling the tougher decisions as you go. And just like peeling an onion, there might be a few tears along the way. But in the end, you're left with something clean, fresh, and ready to use.

Now, I get it—letting go of things isn't always easy. We attach memories, emotions, and even a sense of identity to our belongings. That old sweater? It reminds you of a trip you took years ago. The box of mismatched dishes? They've been in the family forever. But here's the truth: holding onto stuff doesn't keep the memories alive—you do. The memories will stay with you, even if the items don't.

In this chapter, we're going to break down the decluttering process into manageable steps. No more staring at a mountain of stuff and wondering where to start. We'll walk through a room-by-room guide, giving you clear, simple actions to take. We'll discuss how to sort your items effectively, whether you're deciding to keep, donate, sell, or toss. And we'll tackle some of the trickier challenges—like dealing with large items, sentimental collections, and that pesky "I might need this someday" syndrome.

We'll also talk about the emotional side of decluttering. It's not just about stuff; it's about what that stuff represents. We'll explore ways to honor your memories without being weighed down by physical items. And for those moments when it feels too hard to let go, I'll share some strategies to make the process easier and even a little fun.

By the end of this chapter, you'll have a clear path forward. You'll feel lighter, more organized, and ready to embrace the next chapter of your life with less clutter and more freedom. So, roll up your sleeves, grab a box or two, and let's dive in. You've got this.

Room-by-Room Decluttering Guide: Checklists and Worksheets

Decluttering your entire home can feel like a monumental task, but here's a little secret: you don't have to do it all at once. In fact, trying to tackle everything at once is a surefire way to feel overwhelmed. Instead, focus on one room at a time.

To help you stay organized, I've created a simple room-by-room guide filled with practical tips, advice, and step-by-step checklists. You don't have to follow it exactly—feel free to adapt it to your own needs and priorities.

1. The Living Room

The living room is often the heart of the home, which means it can quickly become a catch-all for clutter. From remote controls to old magazines, it's easy for items to pile up without you even noticing. Furniture can also contribute to a cluttered feel if it's outdated, oversized, or no longer serves a purpose.

Practical Tips and Advice:

- **The "One-Year Rule":** If you haven't used or enjoyed something in the past year, it's probably time to let it go.
- **Maximize Storage:** Use baskets or decorative boxes to corral items like remote controls and chargers.
- **Limit Decor:** Choose a few meaningful pieces rather than overcrowding shelves with knickknacks.
- **Evaluate Furniture:** Consider whether each piece of furniture is functional and fits the space. Remove or donate bulky or unnecessary items.
- **Rearrange for Space:** Sometimes simply rearranging furniture can make a room feel larger and more organized.

3-Step Task List:

1. **Clear Surfaces:** Remove everything from coffee tables, shelves, and side tables. Decide what stays and what goes.
2. **Sort and Purge:** Go through books, magazines, DVDs, and small decor items. Donate or recycle anything you no longer enjoy.

3. **Assess Furniture:** Identify pieces that are too big, not used, or don't fit your style. Rearrange or remove them to create a more open and inviting space.

2. The Kitchen

The kitchen can be a tricky space to declutter because it's so functional. However, a clutter-free kitchen makes cooking and cleaning so much easier. When decluttering, also consider your future living situation. If you're moving to an assisted living facility, nursing home, or downsizing to a smaller home, you may not need as many kitchen items.

Practical Tips and Advice:

- **Tackle One Area at a Time:** Focus on one cabinet or drawer before moving on to the next.
- **Check Expiration Dates:** Toss expired spices, canned goods, and other perishables.
- **Limit Duplicates:** Do you really need three can openers or five spatulas?
- **Consider Future Needs:** Think about whether you'll need all your kitchen gadgets and appliances in your new living situation. Assisted living facilities often provide meals, so you may only need a few personal items.
- **Downsize Dishware:** If you're moving to a smaller space, consider keeping only a few plates, cups, and utensils.

3-Step Task List:

1. **Empty Cabinets and Drawers:** Take everything out and assess what you use regularly and what you might need in your new living situation.

2. **Declutter Countertops:** Only keep essential items out, like a coffee maker or toaster, if you'll still need them.

3. **Organize and Label:** Group similar items together, label shelves for easy access, and set aside items to donate or pass on to family if they won't be needed in your next home.

---

3. The Bedroom

Your bedroom should be more than just a place to sleep—it should be a peaceful retreat where you can unwind and recharge. A clutter-free, serene space not only looks inviting but also contributes to better sleep quality and overall relaxation. When your bedroom is free from unnecessary items, it becomes a true sanctuary, helping you start and end your day with a clear mind.

Why Decluttering Your Bedroom Matters:

Clutter can subtly affect your mental state. Piles of clothes, overflowing nightstands, and random items shoved under the bed can create a sense of chaos, even if you don't realize it. On the flip side, a clean and organized bedroom signals to your brain that it's time to relax and rest. Plus, it's much easier to maintain a sleep-friendly environment when things are neat and simple.

Practical Tips and Advice:

• Closet Clean-Out:

When it comes to your closet, it's time to be honest with yourself. If something doesn't fit, hasn't been worn in over a year, or no longer makes you feel confident, it's time to say goodbye. Donate gently used items to someone who will appreciate them, and toss anything that's worn out or beyond repair. You'll be amazed at how much lighter you feel when your closet contains only items you love and actually wear.

• Simplify Nightstands:

Nightstands often become a catch-all for random items—old receipts, chargers, books you never finished, or even empty water glasses. Aim to keep just the essentials: a lamp for reading, a book you're currently enjoying, an alarm clock or phone charger, and perhaps a calming item like a candle or essential oil diffuser. Less clutter means less distraction when it's time to wind down for the night.

• Under-Bed Storage:

The space under your bed is valuable real estate, but it shouldn't become a dumping ground. Use this space intentionally for items like seasonal clothes, spare bedding, or neatly stored keepsakes. Invest in under-bed storage containers or bins to keep things organized and dust-free. Avoid stuffing things haphazardly—it defeats the purpose of creating a clutter-free bedroom.

3-Step Task List:

1. Declutter the Closet:

Pull everything out of your closet and sort it into three piles: *keep*, *donate*, and *toss*. Ask yourself:

- Does this fit me right now?

- Have I worn it in the last year?
- Does it still reflect my style or make me feel good?
  If the answer is *no*, let it go. For sentimental items you can't part with, consider storing them elsewhere to keep your everyday closet space tidy and functional.

2. Tidy Nightstands and Dressers:
Go through your nightstands and dresser tops. Toss out old receipts, empty lotion bottles, and anything else that doesn't belong. Keep surfaces clear, leaving room for just a few meaningful or functional items. For dressers, tidy up drawers by folding clothes neatly and organizing them by type—this will make it easier to find what you need and keep things from getting messy again.

3. Refresh Bedding:
Fresh, clean bedding can make your entire bedroom feel new. Wash your sheets, pillowcases, and comforter, or consider replacing old linens that have seen better days. Fluff your pillows and maybe even rotate your mattress for added comfort. You'd be surprised how much of a difference clean, cozy bedding makes in creating a restful atmosphere.

By following these simple steps, you'll transform your bedroom from a cluttered space into a calm, inviting retreat where you can truly relax. Remember, your bedroom should be a place that feels like a haven, not a storage closet.

---

4. The Bathroom

The bathroom may be one of the smallest rooms in your home, but it's often one of the most cluttered. From expired medications and old beauty products to half-used toiletries and random items you forgot you even owned, bathroom clutter builds up quickly. A tidy, organized bathroom not only looks better but also makes your morning and evening routines more efficient and stress-free.

Why Decluttering Your Bathroom Matters:

Clutter in the bathroom can make even simple tasks feel chaotic. Searching through a mess of products when you're rushing to get ready isn't just frustrating—it can also lead to accidentally using expired or unnecessary items. Plus, bathrooms are high-humidity environments, and cluttered spaces can become breeding grounds for mold and mildew. By decluttering, you'll create a cleaner, healthier, and more pleasant space to start and end your day.

Practical Tips and Advice:

• Toss Expired Items:

Start with the most obvious culprits: expired medications, old skincare, and beauty products. Check expiration dates carefully, especially on items like sunscreen, medications, and cosmetics. Expired products can lose their effectiveness—or worse, become harmful. Dispose of medications safely by following local guidelines or returning them to a pharmacy that accepts them.

• Minimize Duplicates:

It's easy to accumulate multiple bottles of shampoo, conditioners, lotions, and other toiletries, especially if you like to try new products. But do you really need five different types of shampoo or three half-used bottles of the same body wash? Keep the products you actually use and love, and donate or recycle unopened items if possible. Simplifying your product lineup will free up space and make your routine quicker and easier.

• Use Clear Containers:

Clear storage bins or drawer organizers are game-changers for bathroom organization. When you can easily see what you have, you're less likely to overbuy or forget about products. Use small bins or dividers to group similar items—like skincare, hair products, or first-aid supplies. This keeps everything organized and easy to find.

3-Step Task List:

1. Clear Out Cabinets and Drawers:

Start by emptying out every cabinet, drawer, and shelf. Lay everything out on a counter or towel so you can see what you're working with. As you go through each item, ask yourself:

- Is it expired?
- Do I actually use this?
- Does it still work or serve a purpose?

  Toss expired products and dispose of medications properly. For items you haven't used in months—or even years—consider whether you really need them. If not, let them go.

2. Organize Essentials:

Once you've pared things down, organize your remaining essentials. Group similar items together:

- *Daily toiletries*: toothbrush, toothpaste, face wash, etc.

- *Occasional use*: razors, face masks, special treatments.

- *First-aid supplies*: band-aids, antiseptic, over-the-counter meds.

  Use bins or drawer organizers to keep these groups tidy and easily accessible. Consider storing less frequently used items in higher cabinets or less accessible areas to keep your daily essentials front and center.

3. Wipe Down Surfaces:

Before putting anything back, give your bathroom a thorough cleaning. Wipe down counters, mirrors, shelves, and inside drawers or cabinets. This step not only freshens up the space but also prevents dust, residue, or spills from accumulating under your newly organized items. Once everything is sparkling clean, neatly arrange your essentials back in their places.

Bonus Tip:

Consider adopting a "one in, one out" rule for bathroom products. When you buy something new, make sure to finish or dispose of an old product to prevent clutter from creeping back in. This simple habit helps maintain a streamlined, clutter-free bathroom long-term.

By tackling your bathroom clutter, you'll create a space that feels fresh, clean, and calming—making your daily routines smoother and more enjoyable.

5. The Home Office

Your home office should be a space where productivity flourishes, not a clutter magnet for old paperwork, outdated electronics, and random office supplies. A tidy, organized workspace can significantly boost your focus, reduce stress, and make it easier to tackle tasks efficiently. When everything has its place and unnecessary items are cleared away, you'll find yourself feeling more motivated and less overwhelmed.

Why Decluttering Your Home Office Matters:

A cluttered office can lead to a cluttered mind. Visual distractions like piles of paper, tangled cords, and unused gadgets can make it difficult to concentrate. Plus, when your workspace is disorganized, you're more likely to waste time looking for things instead of getting work done. By creating a clean, streamlined environment, you set the stage for increased productivity and a clearer mental space.

Practical Tips and Advice:

• Sort Papers Regularly:

Paper clutter can spiral out of control quickly if left unchecked. Set aside time every week or month to sort through incoming mail, receipts, and documents. Shred anything you no longer need, like old bank statements or outdated bills. For important documents, create a simple filing system—either physical folders or digital scans—that's easy to maintain and access.

• **Declutter Electronics:**
Old gadgets, tangled cords, and obsolete tech accessories have a way of piling up in home offices. Take stock of what you have—are there chargers for devices you no longer own? Keyboards or printers that no longer work? Recycle or donate any electronics you no longer use. For the items you're keeping, label cords and use cable organizers to keep everything neat and tangle-free.

• **Minimize Desk Items:**
Your desk should be a functional space, not a storage surface. Keep only the essentials within arm's reach—a notebook, a pen, your computer, and maybe a small personal touch like a photo or plant. Too many items on your desk can create visual clutter, making it harder to stay focused on the task at hand.

3-Step Task List:

1. Tackle Paper Clutter:

Start by gathering all the papers from your desk, drawers, and any piles that have accumulated. Sort them into categories:

- *Keep*: Important documents like tax records, contracts, or warranties.
- *Shred*: Old bills, sensitive documents, or anything with personal information you no longer need.
- *Recycle*: Non-sensitive papers like old flyers, notes, or junk mail.

Once sorted, file the necessary documents in labeled folders or scan them into a digital system for easy access.

2. Declutter Drawers:

Open each drawer and pull everything out. You'll likely find old pens that don't work, dried-out markers, outdated gadgets, and forgotten office supplies. Toss or recycle anything that's broken or no longer useful. For items you do need, like pens, paperclips, or sticky notes, use drawer organizers to keep them tidy and easy to find.

3. Create a Clean Workspace:

Before putting anything back on your desk, give it a good wipe-down. Clean surfaces help create a fresh start and can even improve your mood while working. Once everything is clean, only put back what you truly need to keep your workspace functional and clutter-free. Keep cables organized and store less frequently used items in drawers or shelves.

Bonus Tip:

Adopt a "reset routine" at the end of each workday. Take a few minutes to clear off your desk, put away any papers or supplies, and prepare your workspace for the next day. This simple habit can help maintain a tidy office and make it easier to dive into work the following morning.

By decluttering your home office, you'll create a space that fosters focus, efficiency, and creativity. A clean workspace is more than just visually appealing—it's a powerful tool for improving your productivity and reducing stress.

6. The Garage, Storage Areas, and Shed

Garages, storage areas, and sheds often become the dumping ground for everything we don't know what to do with—old tools, half-finished projects, forgotten sports equipment, and that random box you meant to sort through years ago. These spaces can feel the most overwhelming to tackle, but they also offer the greatest rewards. By decluttering these areas, you'll free up valuable space, make it easier to find what you need, and even make room for things you actually *use*—like parking your car in the garage again!

Why Decluttering These Spaces Matters:

A cluttered garage or shed can be more than just an eyesore—it can be a safety hazard. Tripping over tools or navigating around piles of stuff isn't just annoying; it's potentially dangerous. Plus, clutter in these areas often hides items you didn't even know you had, leading to unnecessary purchases. By decluttering, you'll save time, money, and frustration while creating a more functional, organized space.

Practical Tips and Advice:

• Categorize Everything:

Before you can declutter, you need to know what you're working with. Sort everything into categories like tools, gardening supplies, sports equipment, holiday decorations, camping gear, and household items. Seeing similar items grouped together will help you realize what you have too much of—and what can be let go.

• Let Go of "Just in Case" Items:

We all hang on to things thinking, *I might need this someday.* But if you haven't used that old power tool, spare piece of wood, or broken lawn chair in the last few years, chances are you won't miss it. Be honest with yourself about what's truly useful and what's just taking up space.

• Use Vertical Space:
When floor space is limited, go vertical. Install shelves, pegboards, or hooks to get items off the ground and neatly stored. Hanging bikes, tools, and even garden hoses on walls can free up tons of space while keeping everything easily accessible. Clear bins or labeled containers on shelves will keep things organized and easy to find.

Don't Forget the Shed and Garden Tools:
If you have a shed, it's likely packed with garden tools, pots, old bags of soil, and who-knows-what-else. Garden tools, in particular, can become rusty, dull, or broken over time. Take a good look at what you have:

- **Keep** tools that are in good shape and serve a purpose.
- **Sharpen or repair** tools that need a little TLC.
- **Toss or recycle** broken, rusted, or duplicate items you no longer use.

Garden tools are one of the first things to get sold at yard sales, especially in the spring, sell the old ones and get new ones if you need them. Smaller items like gloves, seeds, and hand tools can be kept in labeled bins or drawers for easy access.

3-Step Task List:
1. Sort Items into Categories:
Pull everything out of your garage, shed, or storage space. Yes, it might feel overwhelming at first, but seeing everything laid out will help you make better decisions. Group items into categories like:

- *Tools* (power tools, hand tools, etc.)

- *Garden Supplies* (rakes, shovels, pots, soil)
- *Sports Equipment* (bikes, balls, camping gear)
- *Seasonal Decor* (holiday lights, wreaths)
- *Household Items* (paint cans, spare tiles, cleaning supplies)

2. Purge Unused Items:
Once everything is sorted, start purging. Ask yourself:

- *Have I used this in the last year?*
- *Is this item broken or missing parts?*
- *Do I have multiples of this, and do I really need more than one?*

  Donate usable items like sports gear or tools to local charities. Recycle what you can, and responsibly dispose of hazardous materials like old paint, batteries, or chemicals.

3. Organize and Label:
Now that you've cleared out the clutter, it's time to organize what's left. Use shelves, hooks, and pegboards to make the most of your vertical space. Store smaller items in clear bins so you can easily see what's inside, and label everything—this makes it easier to keep the space organized in the future. Consider dedicating specific shelves or zones for each category, so you always know where to find what you need.

Bonus Tip:

Schedule a bi-annual garage and shed check-up. Each spring and fall, take 30 minutes to tidy up, get rid of anything you no longer need, and make sure everything is in its proper place. Regular maintenance will prevent clutter from creeping back in.

Sorting Items: What to Keep, Sell, Donate, or Toss

Once you've started decluttering, the next step is to sort your items into four categories: keep, sell, donate, or toss. Here's how to decide what goes where.

1. Keep

These are the items you use regularly, love deeply, or need for your daily life. Be honest with yourself: if you're keeping something out of guilt or obligation, it might be time to let it go.

2. Sell

If you have items that are still in good condition but no longer serve you, consider selling them. This could include furniture, electronics, or collectibles.

One tip: if you're not sure where to sell something, try online marketplaces like eBay, Facebook Marketplace, or Craigslist.

3. Donate

Donating is a great way to give your items a second life while helping others. Consider donating clothes, household goods, and furniture to local charities or thrift stores.

I'll never forget the story of a man named John, who donated his old tools to a local vocational school. "It felt good to know they'd be put to good use," he told me. "And it was a way to honor my dad's memory"

4. Toss

Finally, there are the items that are broken, expired, or no longer usable. These should be tossed or recycled.

One tip: if you're not sure how to dispose of something, check with your local waste management facility. They can often provide guidance on how to recycle or dispose of items safely.

Dealing with Large Items, Collections, and "I Might Need This Someday" Syndrome

Now, let's tackle some of the trickier aspects of decluttering: large items, collections, and that pesky "I might need this someday" syndrome.

1. Large Items

Large items like furniture, appliances, and exercise equipment can be some of the hardest to let go of. But if they're no longer serving you, it's time to say goodbye.

One tip: if you're struggling to part with a large item, take a photo of it. This way, you can preserve the memory without holding onto the physical object.

2. Collections

Collections can be tricky because they often hold sentimental value. But if your collection is taking up space and no longer bringing you joy, it might be time to let it go.

One tip: consider keeping a few key pieces from your collection and letting go of the rest. This way, you can still enjoy the memories without feeling overwhelmed by the clutter.

3. "I Might Need This Someday" Syndrome

This is perhaps the most common decluttering challenge. We hold onto things because we *might* need them someday—but the truth is, we rarely do.

One tip: if you're holding onto something "just in case," ask yourself how easy it would be to replace if you did need it. If the answer is "pretty easy," it's probably safe to let it go.

Final Thoughts

Decluttering is a journey, and like any journey, it comes with its ups and downs. There will be moments of joy, moments of sadness, and moments of frustration. But through it all, remember this: you're not alone.

In the next chapter, we'll dive into the financial side of downsizing, exploring how to sell your home, avoid common pitfalls, and budget for your new lifestyle. But for now, take a moment to reflect on your decluttering journey. What have you learned about yourself? What memories have you uncovered? And what are you ready to let go of?

Remember, decluttering isn't just about saying goodbye to stuff; it's about making space for what truly matters.

Chapter 5: Financial Aspects of Downsizing

Let's talk about money. I will keep this chapter short as there are plenty of other books out there that can go into far greater detail than what I could do. I don't think I can do it justice in just one chapter. And here's the thing: I'm not here to sell you anything. No hidden agendas, no fancy financial products to push, just honest, practical advice to help you navigate the financial side of this big life change. Think of this as a conversation over coffee, where we're figuring things out together. Because let's face it, downsizing isn't just about clearing out closets and saying goodbye to old furniture—it's about making smart financial decisions that will set you up for a comfortable, stress-free retirement. I feel I can at least cover the basics to get you started.

So, grab a stiff drink and let's dive into the financial aspects of downsizing. We'll cover everything from understanding the financial implications to selling your home and budgeting for your new living situation. And don't worry—I'll keep it real, relatable, and free of any salesy nonsense.

First, let's talk about the potential financial benefits of downsizing. Selling a larger home often means you can free up a significant amount of equity. This can be a game-changer for your retirement savings. Imagine having that extra cushion to travel, spoil the grandkids, or just have peace of mind knowing you're financially secure. But before you start counting those dollars, it's crucial to understand the costs involved in selling your home—real estate agent fees, closing costs, moving expenses, and possible repairs or updates to make your home market-ready. These can add up quickly, so it's important to factor them into your decision.

Next, consider the costs of your new living situation. Downsizing doesn't always mean cheaper. Depending on where you move, you might face higher property taxes, homeowners association (HOA) fees, or even increased utility costs if you're moving to a newer, more energy-efficient home that's in a more expensive area. It's all about balancing what you're saving with what you might be spending.

Budgeting is key here. Create a realistic budget that takes into account not just your new mortgage or rent, but also utilities, insurance, taxes, and day-to-day living expenses. And don't forget to plan for the unexpected—emergency repairs, medical expenses, or those surprise visits from family that somehow always seem to happen at the busiest times.

Finally, think about the long-term financial implications. Downsizing can reduce your monthly expenses and give you more financial freedom, but it's also a chance to reassess your financial goals. Maybe you want to invest some of that freed-up equity, or perhaps you're looking to simplify your financial life as much as your living space.

In the end, downsizing is as much about financial peace of mind as it is about simplifying your home. So, take your time, do the math, and make sure the decisions you make today will set you up for the retirement you've been dreaming of.

Understanding the Financial Implications of Downsizing

First things first: downsizing isn't just about moving to a smaller place. It's about making a financial shift that can have a big impact on your retirement. For many of us, our home is our biggest asset, and selling it can free up a significant amount of money. But before you start dreaming about all the things you could do with that cash, it's important to understand the full picture.

Let's start with the obvious: selling your home. If you've lived in your house for decades, chances are it's appreciated in value. That's great news, but it also means you might be facing a hefty capital gains tax. Now, before you panic, there's some good news here. In many countries, including the U.S., there's a capital gains tax exclusion for primary residences. If you're single, you can exclude up to $250,000 of gains from taxes, and if you're married filing jointly, that number jumps to 250,000 *of gains from taxes, and if you're married filing jointly, that number jumps to* $500,000. That means if your home has appreciated by less than those amounts, you might not owe any taxes at all. But—and this is a big but—you'll want to double-check with a tax professional to make sure you're taking advantage of all the tax benefits available to you.

Now, let's talk about the costs of selling your home. Even if you're not paying capital gains tax, there are still plenty of expenses to consider. Real estate agent commissions, closing costs, moving expenses, and any repairs or upgrades you need to make before putting your home on the market can add up quickly. And don't forget about the emotional cost—because yes, that's a real thing. Letting go of a home filled with memories can be tough, and it's important to factor that into your decision-making process.

On the flip side, downsizing can also lead to significant savings. A smaller home typically means lower utility bills, less maintenance, and potentially lower property taxes. Plus, if you're moving to a retirement community or a condo, you might be able to say goodbye to lawn care, snow removal, and other time-consuming (and expensive) chores. These savings can add up over time, giving you more financial flexibility in retirement.

But here's the thing: downsizing isn't a one-size-fits-all solution. For some people, it makes perfect financial sense. For others, it might not be the best move. That's why it's so important to take a close look at your own financial situation, your goals, and your priorities before making any decisions. And remember, there's no rush. Take your time, do your research, and make sure you're making the choice that's right for you.

Selling Your Home: Choosing Between Agents, FSBO, or Cash Buyers

Okay, so you've decided to sell your home. Now what? Well, the first big decision you'll need to make is how you're going to sell it. And let me tell you, there are a lot of options out there. You can go the traditional route and work with a real estate agent, try your hand at selling it yourself (also known as FSBO, or For Sale By Owner), or even sell to a cash buyer. Each option has its pros and cons, and the right choice for you will depend on your specific situation.

Let's start with real estate agents. If you've sold a home before, you probably already know the drill. A good agent can take a lot of the stress out of the selling process by handling everything from marketing your home to negotiating with buyers. They'll also have access to a network of potential buyers and can help you price your home competitively. But—and this is a big but—real estate agents don't work for free. In most cases, you'll be paying a commission of around 5-6% of the sale price, which can add up to a pretty penny. So, if you're looking to maximize your profits, you might want to consider other options.

That brings us to FSBO, or For Sale By Owner. Selling your home yourself can save you a lot of money on commissions, but it's also a lot of work. You'll be responsible for everything from listing your home to showing it to potential buyers to handling the paperwork. And let's not forget about negotiating with buyers, which can be tricky if you're not experienced. That said, if you're comfortable with the process and willing to put in the time and effort, FSBO can be a great way to keep more money in your pocket.

Finally, there's the option of selling to a cash buyer. This can be a quick and easy way to sell your home, especially if you're in a hurry or don't want to deal with the hassle of traditional selling methods. Cash buyers are typically investors who are looking to buy homes at a discount, so you might not get as much money as you would with a traditional sale. But if speed and convenience are your top priorities, this could be a good option for you.

So, how do you choose? Well, it really comes down to your priorities. If you're looking for a stress-free experience and don't mind paying a commission, a real estate agent might be the way to go. If you're willing to put in the work to save some money, FSBO could be a good fit. And if you're in a hurry or just want to simplify the process, selling to a cash buyer might be your best bet. The key is to weigh the pros and cons of each option and choose the one that aligns with your goals.

Budgeting for Your New Living Situation and Avoiding Common Pitfalls

Once you've sold your home, the next step is figuring out how to budget for your new living situation. This is where a lot of people run into trouble, so it's important to approach this step with care. The last thing you want is to blow through your savings and end up in a tight spot down the road.

First, let's talk about your new home. Whether you're moving to a smaller house, a condo, or a retirement community, you'll need to factor in the cost of your new living situation. This includes not just the purchase price or rent, but also any associated fees, such as homeowners' association (HOA) fees, maintenance costs, and utilities. It's also a good idea to set aside some money for any unexpected expenses that might come up, like repairs or upgrades.

Next, think about your lifestyle. Downsizing often means simplifying, but that doesn't mean you have to give up the things you love. If travel is important to you, make sure to budget for it. If you enjoy dining out or going to the theater, factor those costs into your budget as well. The key is to strike a balance between enjoying your retirement and making sure your money lasts.

One common pitfall to avoid is underestimating your expenses. It's easy to think that downsizing will automatically lead to big savings, but that's not always the case. For example, if you're moving to a more expensive area, your cost of living might actually go up. Or, if you're moving to a retirement community, you might be surprised by the monthly fees. That's why it's so important to do your homework and create a detailed budget before making any big moves.

Another pitfall to watch out for is overspending on your new home. It's tempting to splurge on a fancy new place, but remember, the goal of downsizing is to simplify and save money, not to take on more debt. So, before you start shopping for your dream retirement home, take a close look at your finances and figure out how much you can realistically afford.

Finally, don't forget to plan for the future. Retirement can last decades, so it's important to make sure your money will last as long as you do. This might mean adjusting your budget, investing wisely, or even working part-time to supplement your income. The key is to be proactive and make smart financial decisions now, so you can enjoy a comfortable, stress-free retirement later.

Wrapping It Up

Downsizing is a big decision, and it's not one to be taken lightly. But with a little planning and some careful budgeting, it can also be a smart financial move that sets you up for a comfortable, enjoyable retirement. The key is to take your time, do your research, and make sure you're making the choices that are right for you.

Remember, this is your retirement, and it's all about creating the life you want. So, whether you're selling your home, budgeting for your new living situation, or just trying to figure out how to make your money last, take a deep breath and trust yourself. You've got this. And if you ever need a little extra guidance, don't hesitate to reach out to a financial advisor or other trusted professional. After all, this is your time to enjoy life, and that's exactly what you deserve.

Chapter 6: Practical Tips for Moving

Moving. Just the word can make some of us break out in a cold sweat. It's one of those life events that feels equal parts exciting and overwhelming. But here's the thing: it doesn't have to be a nightmare. In fact, with the right approach, moving can be a smooth, even empowering experience. And that's what we're going to talk about today—how to make your move as stress-free as possible, whether you're downsizing to a cozy condo, moving to a retirement community, or relocating to be closer to family.

So, let's sit down with our coffee (or tea, if that's your preference) and dive into the nitty-gritty of moving. We'll cover everything from choosing the right moving services to packing strategies that won't leave you feeling frazzled. And don't worry—I'll keep it practical, relatable, and free of any unnecessary jargon. After all, this is about making your life easier, not adding more to your plate.

First things first: start early. The moment you know you're going to move, begin planning. Create a timeline and checklist to keep everything organized—trust me, it'll save you a lot of last-minute scrambling. Break down tasks week by week, from sorting through your belongings to scheduling utility transfers. The more you spread out the workload, the less overwhelming it will feel.

When it comes to packing, think of it as an opportunity to declutter. As you go through your things, ask yourself, "Do I really need this?" or "Does this item bring me joy?" If not, consider donating, selling, or gifting it to someone who could use it. Downsizing isn't just about fitting into a smaller space—it's about simplifying your life and keeping only what matters most.

Label your boxes clearly, not just with the room they belong to, but also with a brief description of what's inside. This will make unpacking a breeze and help you find essential items quickly when you arrive at your new home. Keep a separate box for immediate necessities—things like toiletries, a change of clothes, important documents, and some snacks. You'll thank yourself when you don't have to dig through boxes just to find your toothbrush on your first night.

Choosing the right moving service is another critical step. Research different companies, read reviews, and get quotes from at least three movers to compare prices and services. Don't be afraid to ask questions—you want to make sure you're hiring professionals who will treat your belongings with care. If you're considering a DIY move, weigh the pros and cons carefully. It might save money, but it also means more physical work and coordination.

Lastly, give yourself grace throughout the process. Moving can stir up a lot of emotions, especially if you're leaving a home filled with memories. Take time to reflect, reminisce, and even shed a few tears if needed. It's all part of the transition. And remember, every box you pack is a step toward a new chapter filled with new adventures.
By approaching your move with a clear plan and a positive mindset, you can turn what feels like a daunting task into an exciting journey. So, take a deep breath, sip that coffee, and let's get started—one box at a time.

Choosing the Right Moving Services: Senior Move Managers, Estate Sales, and More

Let's start with the big question: who's going to help you move? If you're like most people, your first thought might be to call a traditional moving company. And while that's certainly an option, it's not the only one. In fact, there are specialized services out there designed specifically for seniors, and they can be a game-changer when it comes to reducing stress and simplifying the process.

One of the best-kept secrets in the moving world is the Senior Move Manager. These professionals are like fairy godmothers (or godfathers) for downsizers. They don't just help you pack and move—they can assist with everything from decluttering and organizing to selling unwanted items and even setting up your new home. Imagine walking into your new place and finding your furniture arranged, your pictures hung, and your kitchen stocked with essentials. That's the kind of magic a Senior Move Manager can bring to the table. They are trained to handle the emotional and physical aspects of relocation, offering compassionate support during what can be a challenging time. Many Senior Move Managers are members of the National Association of Senior Move Managers (NASMM), which means they adhere to strict ethical guidelines and standards of practice.
Now, I know what you might be thinking: "That sounds expensive." And yes, hiring a Senior Move Manager is an investment. But when you consider the time, energy, and stress they can save you, it's often worth every penny. Plus, many of these services are customizable, so you can choose the level of help that fits your budget and needs. Whether you need full-service assistance from start to finish or just help with specific tasks like packing or organizing, there's likely a package that suits you.

Another option to consider is an estate sale company. If you're downsizing, chances are you've got a lot of stuff that won't be coming with you to your new home. And while it can be tempting to try to sell everything yourself, the reality is that it's a lot of work. Estate sale companies can handle the entire process for you, from pricing and staging to advertising and running the sale. They'll take a percentage of the proceeds, but in exchange, you get to sit back and let the professionals do the heavy lifting. These companies have the expertise to price items accurately, attract buyers, and maximize your profits—all while saving you the hassle of managing the sale yourself. Some estate sale companies even offer clean-out services, ensuring that your old home is ready for its next occupant.

Of course, if you're more of a DIY person, there's always the option of hiring a traditional moving company or even renting a truck and doing it yourself. Traditional movers can be a good fit if you're comfortable handling the packing and organizing but need assistance with the heavy lifting and transportation. Just keep in mind that moving is physically demanding, and it's okay to ask for help. Whether it's hiring professionals or enlisting family and friends, don't be afraid to lean on others during this transition. Moving can be overwhelming, but with the right support system in place, you can make the process smoother and less stressful.

Ultimately, the right choice depends on your unique situation—your budget, physical capabilities, and emotional readiness for the move. Take the time to explore your options, ask for recommendations, and choose the services that best meet your needs. With the right help, your move can be a positive step toward an exciting new chapter in your life.

Packing Strategies to Avoid Overwhelm

Alright, let's talk about packing. For many of us, this is the most daunting part of the moving process. Where do you even start? How do you decide what to keep, what to donate, and what to toss? And how do you pack everything without losing your mind?

First, take a deep breath. Packing doesn't have to be overwhelming if you approach it with a plan. Here's a strategy that's worked for countless people: start early and tackle one room at a time. Don't wait until the last minute to start packing—give yourself plenty of time to sort through your belongings and make thoughtful decisions. My wife and I took nearly 3 months to pack the last time we moved. We needed every minute of those 3 months too.

Begin with the rooms you use the least, like the guest bedroom or the basement. These spaces are often filled with items you don't need on a daily basis, so packing them up early won't disrupt your routine. As you go through each room, create three piles: keep, donate/sell, and toss. Be honest with yourself about what you really need and what you're holding onto out of habit or sentimentality.

When it comes to packing, labeling is your best friend. Write the contents of each box on the side, along with the room it belongs in. This will make unpacking a breeze and save you from frantically searching for your coffee maker on your first morning in the new place. And don't forget to pack an "essentials" box with the things you'll need right away—think toiletries, a change of clothes, medications, and basic kitchen supplies.

Another tip: downsize as you pack. Moving is the perfect opportunity to let go of things you no longer need or use. That set of dishes you haven't touched in years? Donate it. The stack of old magazines collecting dust in the corner? Recycle them. The goal is to only bring what you truly need and love to your new home.

And here's a little secret: packing can actually be a cathartic experience. As you go through your belongings, you'll likely come across items that bring back fond memories. Take the time to savor those moments and reflect on the life you've built. It's not just about getting rid of stuff—it's about making space for the next chapter of your life.

Now, let's get into some practical strategies that can make the process even smoother.

1. **Set a Packing Schedule:** Break down your packing timeline into manageable chunks. Allocate specific days to tackle each room or category of items. Having a schedule will keep you on track and prevent the last-minute rush that leads to stress.

2. **Gather Supplies Ahead of Time:** Make sure you have all the packing materials you'll need before you start. This includes sturdy boxes, packing tape, bubble wrap, packing paper, and markers. Having everything on hand will save you time and frustration.

3. **Use the Right Size Boxes:** Pack heavier items like books in smaller boxes to make them easier to carry, and lighter items like linens and pillows in larger boxes. This will make moving day less

physically demanding and reduce the risk of boxes breaking.

4. **Pack One Room at a Time:** Focusing on one room at a time helps keep things organized and prevents the process from feeling chaotic. It's also satisfying to see a room completely packed up, giving you a sense of accomplishment.

5. **Color-Code Your Boxes:** Use colored stickers or tape to designate which room each box belongs to. For example, use blue for the kitchen, red for the bedroom, and green for the living room. This visual system will make unloading and unpacking more efficient.

6. **Wrap Breakables Carefully:** Use bubble wrap, packing paper, or even towels and blankets to protect fragile items. Clearly mark these boxes as "FRAGILE" so movers know to handle them with care.

7. **Seal Liquids and Toiletries:** Place items like shampoos, lotions, and cleaning supplies in plastic bags to prevent leaks. It's also a good idea to keep these items separate from electronics and other sensitive belongings.

8. **Take Photos of Electronics:** Before you disconnect your TV, computer, or other electronics, take photos of the wiring setup. This will make it much easier to reconnect everything in your new home without confusion.

9. **Pack an Overnight Bag:** In addition to your essentials box, pack a small bag with everything you'll need for your first night in the new place—pajamas, toiletries, phone charger, and any medications. This way, you won't have to dig through boxes after a long day of moving.

10. **Enlist Help:** Don't be afraid to ask friends or family for help, especially with larger or more difficult items. Just make sure to return the favor or offer them something in appreciation, like a meal or a small gift.

Protecting Important Documents and Valuables

Now, let's talk about something that's easy to overlook but incredibly important: protecting your important documents and valuables during the move. Whether it's your passport, financial records, or family heirlooms, these items are irreplaceable, and you'll want to make sure they're safe and secure.

First, gather all your important documents in one place. This includes things like birth certificates, marriage licenses, wills, medical records, and financial statements. Once you've got everything together, consider investing in a fireproof and waterproof lockbox or safe. This will keep your documents protected not just during the move, but also in your new home.

For valuables like jewelry, family photos, and sentimental items, it's a good idea to keep them with you rather than packing them in the moving truck. These are the things that can't be replaced, so it's worth the extra effort to transport them yourself. If you're flying to your new home, make sure to carry these items in your carry-on luggage rather than checking them.

Another tip: make digital copies of your important documents. Scan or take photos of your IDs, insurance policies, and other critical paperwork, and store them in a secure cloud-based service. That way, if anything gets lost or damaged during the move, you'll still have access to the information you need.
And don't forget about your medical records. If you're moving to a new area, you'll want to make sure your new healthcare providers have access to your medical history. Contact your current doctors and ask them to transfer your records to your new providers. It's a small step that can make a big difference in ensuring a smooth transition.
Finally, consider creating an inventory of your most valuable items. Take photos, note serial numbers, and keep a detailed list of these possessions. This can be incredibly helpful for insurance purposes in case anything gets lost, stolen, or damaged during the move.
By following these strategies, you can take much of the stress out of packing and moving. Remember, it's not just about getting your belongings from one place to another—it's about starting fresh and setting yourself up for success in your new home. So, take it one step at a time, stay organized, and don't be afraid to ask for help when you need it. Happy moving!
Final Thoughts: Making the Move Your Own
Moving is a big deal, and it's okay to feel a mix of emotions as you go through the process. Excitement, sadness, anxiety, hope—it's all part of the journey. The key is to give yourself grace and take things one step at a time. Change, no matter how positive, can feel overwhelming. It's normal to have moments of doubt or nostalgia, especially if you're leaving a home filled with years of memories. But remember, those memories aren't tied to the walls—they're part of you and will come with you wherever you go.

Remember, this is your move, and you get to do it your way. Whether that means hiring a Senior Move Manager to handle the details or enlisting your grandkids to help you pack, there's no right or wrong way to do it. You might prefer meticulously labeling every box or taking a more relaxed approach, sorting as you go. The goal is to create a transition that feels manageable and even enjoyable. Don't be afraid to ask for help when you need it—friends and family are often more than willing to lend a hand, and their support can make the process feel less daunting.

And don't forget to celebrate along the way. Moving is a milestone, and it's worth taking a moment to acknowledge all the hard work you've put into making this change. Whether it's treating yourself to a nice dinner, hosting a small farewell gathering with neighbors, or simply taking a moment to sit back and admire your progress, find ways to reward yourself for the effort you're putting in. These small celebrations can help mark the transition and make the process feel more positive.

So, as you embark on this next chapter, remember: you've got this. With a little planning, a lot of patience, and a dash of humor, you'll be settling into your new home before you know it. Take time to explore your new surroundings, meet your neighbors, and create new routines that make your space feel like home. And who knows? You might even find that moving isn't so bad after all. It might open doors to new friendships, experiences, and opportunities you hadn't imagined.

Chapter 7: Adjusting to Your New Space

So, you've done it. You've decluttered, downsized, and moved into your new space. Congratulations! This is a huge accomplishment, and you should be proud of yourself. But now comes the next phase: adjusting to your new home and making it truly feel like yours.

Let's be honest—moving to a smaller space can feel like a big adjustment, especially if you've lived in the same house for decades. Suddenly, you're surrounded by fewer belongings, a different layout, and maybe even a new neighborhood. It's natural to feel a little disoriented at first. But here's the good news: with a little time, effort, and creativity, you can turn this new space into a place that feels just as warm and welcoming as your old home.

Start by personalizing your space. Displaying your favorite photos, artwork, or keepsakes can instantly make a room feel more familiar. Even in a smaller space, you can find creative ways to showcase the items that matter most to you. Consider using floating shelves, multi-purpose furniture, or wall-mounted organizers to keep things tidy while adding a personal touch.

Next, establish new routines that help you settle in. Maybe you'll find a cozy corner for your morning coffee or discover a local park for your daily walks. These small rituals can bring a sense of comfort and stability. Take time to explore your new neighborhood—visit local shops, meet your neighbors, and find new favorite spots. Building connections in your community can make a big difference in how quickly you feel at home.

Staying organized is key to preventing clutter from creeping back in. Make it a habit to regularly evaluate your belongings and let go of items you no longer need. Embrace storage solutions that maximize your space, like under-bed storage bins, stackable containers, or closet organizers. Remember, the goal is to maintain a space that feels open, functional, and inviting.

Finally, give yourself grace during this transition. It's okay if it takes time to fully adjust—moving is a big life change, and it's normal to experience a mix of emotions. Celebrate the progress you've made and focus on the exciting opportunities this new chapter brings. With patience and a positive mindset, you'll soon find that your new space isn't just a house—it's home.

In this chapter, we'll talk about how to make a smaller space feel like home, stay organized so you don't fall back into clutter, and embrace the new routines and opportunities that come with this next chapter of your life.

Making a Smaller Space Feel Like Home

One of the biggest challenges of downsizing is figuring out how to make a smaller space feel cozy and inviting. After all, you're not just moving into a new home—you're creating a new lifestyle. And while it might feel strange at first, there are plenty of ways to make your new space feel like you.

Start with Thoughtful Furniture Choices

First, let's talk about furniture. When you're moving to a smaller space, it's important to choose pieces that are both functional and meaningful. Instead of trying to cram all your old furniture into the new place, take the time to carefully select the items that truly matter to you. Maybe it's the armchair you've had for years, the dining table where your family gathers for holidays, or the bookshelf that holds your favorite reads. These are the pieces that will make your new space feel like home because they carry memories and comfort.

But here's a tip: scale down where you can. A massive sectional sofa might have worked in your old living room, but it could overwhelm a smaller space. Look for furniture that's proportionate to your new home, like a loveseat instead of a full couch or a drop-leaf table that can expand when you need it but stay compact when you don't. And don't forget about multi-functional pieces, like ottomans with hidden storage, a bed with built-in drawers, or nesting tables that can be tucked away when not in use. These clever pieces can be lifesavers in a smaller space, helping you maximize storage without feeling cluttered.

Let Your Personality Shine with Decor

Next, let's talk about decor. This is where you can really let your personality shine and make the space feel uniquely yours. Hang up your favorite artwork, display family photos, and add touches of color with throw pillows, rugs, and curtains. Even small items like a cherished vase, a quirky clock, or a handmade quilt can infuse your space with warmth and familiarity. These details might seem minor, but they create an environment that feels lived-in and loved.

Think about using vertical space, too. Wall-mounted shelves or hooks can display decorative items or store essentials without taking up floor space. Mirrors are another great tool—they can make a room feel larger and reflect light to brighten darker corners.

And if you always wanted a leather couch, buy the damned leather couch. Don't worry if the dog or cat will scratch it up, it's probably the last couch you will ever own. Buy a comfortable one that you enjoy sitting in.

The Power of Good Lighting

And don't forget about lighting. Good lighting can completely transform a space, making it feel brighter, bigger, and more welcoming. If your new home doesn't get a lot of natural light, consider adding floor lamps, table lamps, or even string lights to create a cozy atmosphere. Layer your lighting by combining ambient (overhead), task (reading lamps), and accent lighting (to highlight artwork or decor). Warm-toned bulbs can add to the cozy feel, while dimmable lights let you adjust the mood to fit different occasions.

Embrace the Adjustment Period

Finally, give yourself time to adjust. It's normal to feel a little out of place at first, especially if you're used to a larger home with more room to spread out. Downsizing isn't just about the physical space—it's about shifting your mindset and embracing a simpler, more streamlined lifestyle. Over time, as you settle in, personalize the space, and create new routines, it will start to feel more and more like home. And you might even find that the cozy, efficient space becomes your favorite place to be.

Remember, home isn't about square footage—it's about the people, memories, and feelings you bring into it. With a little creativity and patience, your smaller space can be just as warm, inviting, and fulfilling as any larger home.

Embracing New Routines, Building Social Networks, and Finding Community

One of the most exciting aspects of downsizing is the opportunity to embrace a new lifestyle. Whether you've moved to a new city, a retirement community, or just a smaller home in the same area, this is your chance to create new routines, build new relationships, and find a sense of community.

Let's start with routines. Moving to a new space often means adjusting to a new daily rhythm. Maybe you're no longer responsible for maintaining a large yard, or perhaps you're living closer to amenities like parks, libraries, or coffee shops. Take advantage of these changes to create routines that bring you joy and fulfillment.

For example, if you've always wanted to start your day with a walk, now's the perfect time to make it a habit. Enjoy the fresh air, explore your new surroundings, and perhaps even discover a favorite route. If you've been dreaming of spending more time on hobbies like painting, gardening, or reading, carve out time in your schedule to do just that. A smaller home often means less time spent on upkeep, freeing you up to focus on what truly matters to you. The key is to create routines that reflect your priorities and values. Whether it's a morning meditation, an afternoon at the local coffee shop with a good book, or an evening stroll through the neighborhood, find what brings you peace and satisfaction.

Next, let's talk about building social networks. Moving to a new place can feel isolating at first, especially if you've left behind friends and neighbors. But it's also an opportunity to meet new people and form new connections. Building a social network doesn't have to be daunting—it can be as simple as striking up a conversation with someone at the local farmer's market or attending a community event.

My best advice is get off that brand new couch and go out and join some clubs, go to the local senior or community center and sign up for new activities. Start by getting involved in your community. Join a local club or organization that aligns with your interests, whether it's a gardening group, a book club, or a fitness class. Attend events at your neighborhood library or community center, where you can engage with people who share your passions. Volunteering for a cause you care about is another wonderful way to meet like-minded individuals while making a positive impact.

If you've moved to a retirement community, take advantage of the social opportunities that are often available. Many communities offer activities like exercise classes, book clubs, and game nights, which can be a fun way to meet your neighbors and stay active. Don't be afraid to step out of your comfort zone and try something new—you might discover a hidden talent or a new favorite pastime.

And don't forget about technology. If you're not already familiar with video calling platforms like Zoom or FaceTime, now's a great time to learn. These tools can help you stay connected with family and friends, even if they're far away. Social media platforms and online forums tailored to your interests can also be valuable resources for connecting with others, sharing experiences, and even finding local events.

Maintaining connections with old friends is just as important as making new ones. Regular phone calls, video chats, or even handwritten letters can keep those bonds strong, no matter the distance. Consider setting up regular virtual meetups, like a monthly book club or a weekly coffee chat, to maintain a sense of continuity with your loved ones.

Finally, be patient with yourself. Building a new social network takes time, and it's okay if it doesn't happen overnight. Focus on taking small steps, like introducing yourself to a neighbor or attending a local event, and let things unfold naturally. Remember that it's perfectly normal to feel a mix of excitement and uncertainty when adjusting to a new environment. Give yourself grace as you navigate these changes, and trust that with time, you'll find your rhythm and your people.

Downsizing isn't just about moving to a smaller space—it's about creating a lifestyle that aligns with your current needs and future goals. Embrace the opportunities that come with this transition, and you'll find that a smaller home can lead to a richer, more fulfilling life. Whether through new routines, meaningful connections, or a strong sense of community, the possibilities are endless.

Final Thoughts: Embracing the Next Chapter

Adjusting to a new space is about more than just unpacking boxes and arranging furniture. It's about creating a new way of life—one that reflects who you are and what you value most.

As you settle into your new home, remember to give yourself grace. It's okay to feel a little out of place at first, and it's okay to miss your old home. Change is never easy, but it's also an opportunity for growth and renewal. Every picture you hang, every cozy nook you create, and every memory you make will slowly transform this house into your sanctuary.

Take time to explore your new surroundings. Discover the local coffee shop where the barista remembers your name, stroll through nearby parks, or attend community events—these small experiences will help you feel connected and rooted in your new environment. Embrace the chance to reinvent your routines and let go of things that no longer serve you, both physically and emotionally.

So, take a deep breath and embrace this next chapter. Whether you're making your new space feel like home, staying organized, or building new connections, know that you're not alone. This is your time to create a life that's filled with joy, purpose, and meaning.

And who knows? You might just find that this new space feels more like home than you ever imagined. With patience and an open heart, you'll discover that every transition brings hidden treasures—new friendships, fresh perspectives, and unexpected joys.

Here's to new beginnings, fresh starts, and the exciting adventures that lie ahead. Cheers!

Chapter 8: Coping with Change and Letting Go

Let's get real for a moment. Downsizing isn't just about sorting through stuff or moving to a smaller space. It's about change—big, life-altering change. And change, even when it's positive, can be hard. It can stir up emotions you didn't expect, from sadness and nostalgia to anxiety and even guilt. If you've been feeling this way, let me assure you: you're not alone.

This chapter is all about the emotional side of downsizing. We're going to dive deep into the feelings that come with letting go of a home you've loved, the memories tied to your belongings, and the life you've built over the years. But we're also going to talk about how to honor those memories while embracing the new opportunities ahead. This isn't about moving on and forgetting—it's about moving forward with intention and grace.

So, let's have an honest, heartfelt conversation about coping with change and letting go.

First, let's acknowledge something important: it's okay to feel a mix of emotions during this process. You might be excited about a fresh start, but at the same time, you might feel a deep sense of loss. That's natural. After all, your home isn't just four walls and a roof—it's where you've lived your life, celebrated milestones, and weathered storms. Each room holds stories, and each object carries a memory. It's no wonder that letting go can feel overwhelming.

One of the first steps in coping with this change is to give yourself permission to feel. Don't rush through the process or brush off your emotions as unimportant. Allow yourself to grieve the loss of your old home and the chapter of life it represents. Grieving doesn't mean you're not ready for what's next—it means you're honoring your past while making space for your future. You might find it helpful to share your feelings with someone you trust. Talking to a friend, family member, or counselor can provide a safe space to process your emotions. Sometimes, just voicing your thoughts can bring clarity and relief. If you're part of a community or support group, consider sharing your experiences there. You'll likely find that others are going through similar transitions and can offer valuable insights and encouragement.

Another key part of coping with change is reframing your perspective. Instead of focusing solely on what you're losing, try to think about what you're gaining. Downsizing can bring freedom—freedom from the burden of maintaining a large home, from clutter, and from the weight of things you no longer need. It can open up opportunities for new experiences, relationships, and adventures. It's a chance to simplify your life and focus on what truly matters.

That said, letting go of physical belongings can be particularly tough. Objects often hold sentimental value because they're tied to memories and people we love. When you find it hard to part with something, ask yourself: Does this item bring me joy? Do I use it regularly? Is it serving a purpose in my life right now? If the answer is no, it might be time to let it go. But that doesn't mean you have to forget the memories associated with it.

One strategy is to take photos of items before you let them go. This way, you can preserve the memory without holding onto the physical object. You might also consider keeping a journal where you write about the stories and emotions connected to certain belongings. Sharing these stories with loved ones can be a beautiful way to honor your past while creating new memories together.

Another approach is to pass cherished items on to family and friends. Knowing that your belongings will be appreciated and used by someone you care about can make it easier to part with them. It's a way of keeping the memory alive while letting go of the physical attachment.

Celebrate small victories along the way, whether it's clearing out a closet, donating items to charity, or simply acknowledging your progress. Each step forward is a testament to your resilience and courage.

Lastly, embrace the idea that downsizing is not just an ending—it's a new beginning. It's a chance to design a life that aligns with your current needs and desires. Think about the opportunities that lie ahead: more time for hobbies and interests, the possibility of travel, or the freedom to explore new communities and relationships. This is your time to create a space and a life that reflects who you are today.

In the end, coping with change and letting go is about finding balance. It's about honoring your past while looking forward to the future with hope and excitement. It's about recognizing that while the physical space and objects may change, the memories and experiences that shaped you will always be a part of who you are.

So take a deep breath, give yourself grace, and trust that you have the strength to navigate this transition. You're not just downsizing your home—you're opening the door to new possibilities, and that's something to celebrate.

Strategies for Managing the Emotional Impact of Downsizing

Let's start by acknowledging something important: downsizing is emotional. It's not just about the physical act of packing up your home; it's about saying goodbye to a place that holds so many memories. Maybe it's the house where you raised your kids, the kitchen where you hosted countless family dinners, or the garden you spent years nurturing. Letting go of that can feel like letting go of a part of yourself.

And that's okay. It's okay to feel sad, nostalgic, or even a little lost. These emotions are a natural part of the process, and they don't mean you're making the wrong decision. In fact, they're a sign that you've lived a full, meaningful life in this space.

So, how do you manage these emotions? Here are a few strategies that might help:

1. **Give Yourself Permission to Feel**

   It's easy to push emotions aside, especially when you're busy with the logistics of moving. But ignoring your feelings can make them harder to deal with in the long run. Instead, give yourself permission to feel whatever comes up. If you need to cry, cry. If you need to laugh at the absurdity of it all, laugh. There's no right or wrong way to feel during this process.

2. **Create a Memory Box**
   As you go through your belongings, you'll likely come across items that hold special meaning but don't have a place in your new home. Instead of letting them go completely, consider creating a memory box. Fill it with photos, letters, small mementos, and other items that remind you of your life in this home. It's a tangible way to hold onto the memories without holding onto the clutter.

3. **Celebrate the Milestones**
   Moving out of your home is a milestone, and it's worth celebrating. Host a farewell gathering with family and friends, or take a moment to walk through each room and reflect on the memories you've made there. You could even write a letter to your home, thanking it for the shelter, comfort, and joy it's provided over the years.

4. **Lean on Your Support System**
   You don't have to go through this alone. Reach out to family, friends, or a therapist if you're feeling overwhelmed. Sometimes, just talking about what you're going through can make a world of difference.

5. **Focus on What You're Gaining**
   While it's natural to focus on what you're leaving behind, try to shift your perspective to what you're gaining. Maybe downsizing means less

maintenance and more free time. Perhaps it allows you to move closer to family or to a community where you can make new friends. Focusing on these positive aspects can help balance the sense of loss.

6. **Establish New Traditions**
Moving to a new place offers an opportunity to create new traditions. Maybe you start hosting a weekly dinner with neighbors or take up a new hobby that's easier to pursue in your new space. Establishing new routines can help you feel more grounded and excited about this next chapter.

7. **Keep a Journal**
Writing down your thoughts and feelings can be incredibly therapeutic. A journal gives you a private space to process your emotions, reflect on your experiences, and track your progress. You might even find that writing helps you uncover feelings you weren't fully aware of.

8. **Take Your Time**
There's no rule that says you have to rush through the process of letting go. If you're not ready to part with certain items, that's okay. Give yourself permission to move at your own pace. Downsizing is a journey, not a race.

9. **Seek Professional Help if Needed**
If you find that the emotional weight of downsizing is too much to handle on your own, don't hesitate to seek professional help. Therapists and counselors can provide valuable

support and coping strategies tailored to your specific situation.

10. **Visualize Your New Space**
    Take some time to imagine what your new home will look and feel like. Visualizing yourself happy and comfortable in your new space can help ease the transition. Consider creating a vision board with pictures and ideas that inspire you.

11. **Stay Connected to Your Old Life**
    Just because you're moving doesn't mean you have to sever all ties with your past. Keep in touch with neighbors and friends from your old community. Visit familiar places when you can. Staying connected can provide a sense of continuity and comfort.

12. **Practice Gratitude**
    Make it a habit to focus on the things you're grateful for, both from your past and in your new life. Gratitude can shift your mindset and help you find peace during times of change. Each day, write down three things you're thankful for—big or small.

Remember, it's not about erasing the past—it's about making space for the future. And that's a process, not a one-time event. Be patient with yourself as you navigate these emotions. Downsizing may feel overwhelming at times, but it's also an opportunity for growth, renewal, and new adventures. By embracing the emotional journey, you can find a deeper sense of fulfillment and excitement for what lies ahead.

In the end, managing the emotional impact of downsizing is about finding balance—honoring your past while looking forward to your future with hope and enthusiasm. You're closing one chapter, but you're also opening the door to new possibilities.

Letting Go Without Losing Memories

One of the hardest parts of downsizing is letting go of belongings that are tied to memories. That old rocking chair might not fit in your new living room, but it's the chair you rocked your babies in. The china set might be too formal for your new lifestyle, but it's the set you used for holiday dinners with your family. How do you let go of these things without feeling like you're losing a piece of your history?

Here's the thing: memories don't live in objects. They live in you. Letting go of a physical item doesn't mean you're letting go of the memory itself. But I get it—that's easier said than done. So, here are some ways to honor your memories while still decluttering:

1. **Take Photos**

   If there's an item you're attached to but can't keep, take a photo of it. You could even create a digital or physical photo album of these items, along with a note about why they're meaningful to you. This way, you can revisit the memories whenever you want, without the physical clutter.

2. **Pass It On**

   Sometimes, the best way to let go of an item is to pass it on to someone who will cherish it as much as you did. That rocking chair could become a treasured heirloom for your grandchild, and the china set could go to a young couple just starting their own family traditions. Knowing that these items are being loved and used can make it easier to part with them.

3. **Create a Memory Ritual**
   For items that feel especially hard to let go of, consider creating a small ritual to honor them. Light a candle, say a few words of gratitude, or simply take a moment to reflect on what the item meant to you. This can help you feel a sense of closure and peace.

4. **Focus on the Essence**
   Think about what the item represents. Maybe that old quilt reminds you of cozy winter nights with your family. Instead of keeping the quilt itself, you could recreate the feeling by knitting a new blanket or hosting a family game night in your new home. It's not about the object—it's about the essence of what it represents.

5. **Document Your Stories**
   Sometimes, the most valuable part of an item is the story it holds. Take the time to write down the history of your cherished belongings—where they came from, who gave them to you, and the memories tied to them. You can create a personal journal or even record these stories as audio files for future generations to listen to. This way, the memories live on, even if the items don't.

6. **Mix Old with New**
   In your new home, try blending old cherished items with new ones. This can create a sense of continuity and help you feel grounded in both

your past and present. Maybe you display your grandmother's vase on a new shelf or use an old family tablecloth during modern gatherings. This approach allows you to carry your history into your future.

Letting go is never easy, but it can be a deeply meaningful process. It's a chance to reflect on the life you've lived and the people and experiences that have shaped you. And it's an opportunity to carry those memories forward in a way that feels authentic and intentional.

Honoring the Past While Creating New Traditions in Your New Home

As you settle into your new space, you might find yourself missing the rhythms and routines of your old life. Maybe you miss the way the sunlight streamed through your kitchen window in the morning, or the sound of the neighborhood kids playing outside. These little things can feel like a big loss, and it's okay to grieve them.

But here's the beautiful thing: your new home is a blank canvas. It's a chance to honor the past while creating new traditions and memories. Here's how you can do that:

1. **Bring Pieces of the Past with You**
   While you can't bring everything with you, you can bring a few meaningful items that help your new space feel like home. Maybe it's a piece of artwork, a favorite quilt, or a collection of family photos. These items can serve as a bridge between your old life and your new one.

2. **Recreate Your Favorite Rituals**
   Think about the rituals and traditions that brought you joy in your old home, and find ways

to recreate them in your new space. If you loved hosting Sunday dinners, invite your family or new neighbors over for a meal. If you enjoyed gardening, start a small container garden on your balcony or patio. These familiar rhythms can help you feel grounded and connected.

3. **Explore Your New Community**
   One of the best ways to feel at home in a new place is to get to know the people and places around you. Take a walk around your neighborhood, visit a local café, or join a community group. The more you explore, the more you'll start to feel like you belong.

4. **Create New Traditions**
   Your new home is an opportunity to try new things and create new traditions. Maybe it's a weekly movie night, a monthly potluck with friends, or a yearly trip to a nearby park. These new rituals can help you build a sense of joy and belonging in your new space.

5. **Celebrate the Journey**
   Finally, take time to celebrate this new chapter of your life. Whether it's a housewarming party, a quiet moment of reflection, or a toast to new beginnings, find a way to mark this transition and acknowledge how far you've come.

6. **Create a Comfort Corner**
   Set up a special spot in your new home that feels like a sanctuary. This could be a reading nook, a cozy chair with a favorite blanket, or a small

corner filled with personal mementos. Having a dedicated space where you can relax and feel at peace can make your new environment feel more comforting and familiar.

7. **Stay Connected with Loved Ones**
   Maintaining strong relationships with family and friends from your old neighborhood can help ease the transition. Regular phone calls, video chats, or planned visits can keep you connected to your roots while you build new connections in your new community.

8. **Reflect on Your Growth**
   Moving to a new home is not just a physical shift; it's an emotional and personal journey as well. Take time to reflect on how you've grown through the process. Consider keeping a journal where you document your feelings, challenges, and successes as you adapt to your new surroundings.

9. **Embrace Change with an Open Mind**
   Change can be intimidating, but it can also be invigorating. Approach your new home and community with curiosity and an open heart. Be willing to step out of your comfort zone and try new experiences. This openness can lead to unexpected joys and discoveries.

10. **Share Your New Space**
    Invite friends and family over to share your new home. Hosting gatherings, no matter how small, can infuse your space with warmth and laughter.

It's a wonderful way to create new memories while honoring the relationships that have been part of your journey.

By honoring the past and embracing the future, you can create a rich tapestry of memories that reflect the full spectrum of your life's experiences. Downsizing and moving don't mean leaving behind who you are; they're opportunities to carry forward the essence of your history while building new, meaningful traditions.

Final Thoughts: Embracing the Beauty of Change

Change is never easy, but it's also one of the most beautiful parts of life. It's a reminder that we're always growing, evolving, and becoming more of who we're meant to be. Downsizing is a big change, but it's also an opportunity—to simplify, to reflect, and to create a life that's aligned with your values and priorities.

As you navigate this transition, remember to be kind to yourself. It's okay to feel a mix of emotions, and it's okay to take your time. This is your journey, and there's no right or wrong way to do it.

And most importantly, remember that you're not saying goodbye to the past—you're carrying it with you, in your heart and in your memories. At the same time, you're opening yourself up to new possibilities, new connections, and new joys.

Change invites us to step outside of our comfort zones and into the unknown. It's in these moments of uncertainty that we discover our true strength and resilience. Downsizing isn't just about letting go of physical items—it's about embracing a new way of living that brings clarity, freedom, and intentionality into our lives.

One of the gifts of downsizing is the ability to focus on what truly matters. When we strip away the excess, we make room for deeper connections, meaningful experiences, and personal growth. It's a chance to realign with your values and prioritize the things that bring you joy and fulfillment.

Think of this as a new chapter in your life story. Every chapter before has shaped you into the person you are today, and every chapter ahead holds new adventures waiting to unfold. Your past is the foundation that supports your future—and while the setting may change, the essence of who you are remains constant.

As you settle into your new space, take time to appreciate the small moments of beauty around you. The morning light streaming through new windows, the quiet peace of a simplified home, and the opportunities that come with meeting new neighbors or exploring a different community. These moments, though small, are the building blocks of your new life.

Remember, it's natural to have moments of doubt or nostalgia. You might find yourself missing familiar routines or feeling sentimental about the home you left behind. Allow yourself to feel these emotions without judgment—they're a testament to the rich life you've lived. But also, give yourself permission to be excited about the future. Every ending is also a beginning, and every goodbye makes space for a new hello.

Surround yourself with people who uplift and support you during this transition. Whether it's family, friends, or new neighbors, having a strong support system can make all the difference. Share your journey with others, celebrate your milestones, and don't hesitate to lean on loved ones when you need a listening ear or a helping hand.

Take this opportunity to rediscover passions and interests that may have taken a backseat in your busy life. Maybe there's a hobby you've always wanted to pursue, a place you've wanted to visit, or a skill you've wanted to learn. Downsizing can free up not just physical space, but also time and energy to invest in the things that light you up. Consider setting new goals for this next phase of your life. These don't have to be grand or ambitious—sometimes the simplest goals bring the most joy. It could be as straightforward as spending more time outdoors, connecting with your community, or dedicating time each day to something that brings you peace.

Embrace the changes in your environment as an opportunity to cultivate a sense of mindfulness. Being present in the moment allows you to fully experience the richness of your new life. Notice the details—the way your new home smells, the sounds of your neighborhood, the feeling of starting fresh. These sensory experiences can ground you and help you appreciate the beauty of the present.

As you move forward, remember that your home is more than just a place—it's a reflection of your journey, your values, and your heart. Fill it with things that bring you joy, surround yourself with people who inspire you, and create spaces that nurture your well-being. Let your new home be a sanctuary where you can continue to grow, thrive, and find peace.

Change may come with challenges, but it also brings opportunities for growth and transformation. Each step you take is a testament to your courage and resilience. Trust in your ability to navigate this journey with grace and confidence. You have already accomplished so much, and there's a world of possibilities waiting for you.

Chapter 9: Special Downsizing Scenarios

Life is full of twists and turns, and downsizing is no exception. While the idea of moving to a smaller home is one thing, there are certain situations that add layers of complexity—and emotion—to the process. Maybe you're considering a move into assisted living, or perhaps you're planning to live with family for the first time in decades. Or maybe you're making a long-distance move, leaving behind a community you've called home for years. These scenarios come with their own unique challenges, but they also offer opportunities for growth, connection, and new beginnings. In this chapter, we'll explore these special downsizing situations with empathy and practicality. We'll talk about how to navigate the emotional and logistical hurdles, make the transition as smooth as possible, and find joy in the journey.

Moving into Assisted Living

Transitioning into an assisted living facility is a significant life change. It's not just about moving to a smaller space; it's about adjusting to a new lifestyle, new routines, and sometimes, new limitations. This can be an emotional process, as it often symbolizes a shift in independence. However, it's also an opportunity to embrace a community of peers, access professional care, and simplify daily living.

When preparing for this move, start by visiting potential facilities. Take note of the atmosphere, staff interactions, and available amenities. Speak with current residents if possible to get a sense of the community vibe. Once you've chosen a facility, work on downsizing your belongings thoughtfully. Focus on keeping items that bring comfort and familiarity—family photos, a favorite armchair, cherished mementos—while letting go of what's no longer needed.

Emotionally, it helps to reframe this transition as a step toward a supportive environment where new friendships and experiences await. Involve family and friends in the process to make it feel less daunting and more like a shared journey.

Moving in with Family

Living with family after years of independence can be both rewarding and challenging. Whether you're moving in with adult children, siblings, or other relatives, it's essential to set clear expectations from the beginning. Discuss household responsibilities, personal space, and financial contributions openly to avoid misunderstandings later.

This living arrangement can foster deeper family bonds and provide emotional support, but it's important to maintain a sense of individuality. Bring along personal items that reflect your personality and help create a space that feels like your own within the larger household. Establish routines that give you a sense of purpose and autonomy.

Communication is key. Regular family meetings can help address any issues that arise and ensure everyone feels heard and respected. Embrace the opportunity to create new memories while honoring each person's need for space and independence.

Long-Distance Moves

Relocating to a new city or state later in life can be both exciting and overwhelming. Whether you're moving to be closer to family, seeking a better climate, or pursuing a dream location, long-distance moves require careful planning.

Start by researching your new community thoroughly. Visit if possible, and explore neighborhoods, healthcare options, and local amenities. Consider the cost of living and how it aligns with your retirement budget. Once you've chosen your new home, plan your move in stages. Downsizing before a long-distance move can reduce both costs and stress, so be selective about what you bring. Emotionally, leaving behind a familiar community can be tough. Acknowledge the grief that may come with saying goodbye to friends, neighbors, and routines. Stay connected through phone calls, video chats, and visits when possible. At the same time, look forward to the opportunities that await—new friendships, activities, and experiences that can enrich this next chapter of life.

Navigating the Emotional Landscape

Regardless of the specific downsizing scenario, emotions will play a significant role in the process. It's natural to feel a mix of excitement, sadness, anxiety, and hope. Give yourself permission to grieve the changes while also embracing the possibilities ahead.

One helpful approach is to focus on the 'why' behind your move. Whether it's for better care, closer family connections, or new adventures, keeping your purpose in mind can provide clarity and motivation. Celebrate small milestones along the way, and don't hesitate to seek support from friends, family, or professionals if needed.

Finding Joy in the Journey

While downsizing can be challenging, it's also an opportunity to simplify, refocus, and rediscover what truly matters. It's a chance to curate your living space with intention, surrounding yourself with items and people that bring joy and comfort.

Approach this transition with an open heart and mind. Embrace the new experiences, relationships, and routines that come with change. Remember, downsizing isn't just about letting go—it's about making room for what's next.

Whether you're facing one of these situations yourself or supporting a loved one who is, this chapter is here to help. Together, we'll navigate the journey with empathy, practical tips, and a spirit of optimism.

Moving into Assisted Living or a Senior Care Community

Let's start with one of the most common—and often most emotional—downsizing scenarios: moving into assisted living or a senior care community. This decision often comes with a mix of feelings, from relief and excitement to sadness and uncertainty. After all, it's not just a move—it's a significant life transition that can stir up a whirlwind of emotions and thoughts.

First, let's acknowledge the emotions. It's natural to feel a sense of loss when leaving a home you've loved, especially if it's been a place of independence and autonomy. You might worry about losing your sense of self or your connection to the life you've built. Memories of family gatherings, holiday celebrations, and quiet moments in your favorite chair might flood your mind. These feelings are valid, and it's important to give yourself permission to feel them. Grieving the loss of your old home is part of the process, and it's okay to take the time you need to adjust.

At the same time, it's worth focusing on the positives. Assisted living and senior care communities offer a level of support and social connection that can be incredibly enriching. Many people find that they thrive in these environments, enjoying activities, making new friends, and having peace of mind knowing that help is available if needed. These communities often provide opportunities for learning new skills, engaging in hobbies, and participating in events that you might not have had access to before. Whether it's joining a book club, taking an art class, or enjoying regular social gatherings, there are countless ways to stay active and connected.

Here are some practical tips to make the transition smoother:

1. **Involve Loved Ones in the Process**
   Moving into assisted living is a big decision, and it's okay to lean on your family and friends for support. They can help you research options, visit communities, and even assist with the downsizing process. Having their involvement can make the transition feel less overwhelming. Talk openly with your loved ones about your feelings and concerns—they can provide emotional support and reassurance. Plus, involving them in the process can help them feel more connected and supportive of your new journey.

2. **Take Your Time Choosing a Community**
   Not all senior care communities are the same, so it's important to find one that feels like the right fit. Visit multiple places, ask lots of questions, and pay attention to how you feel during your visits. Do the staff seem kind and attentive? Do the residents seem happy and engaged? Are the

facilities clean, safe, and welcoming? Trust your instincts. It's also helpful to visit at different times of the day to get a full picture of the daily routine and atmosphere. Remember, this is your new home—it should feel comfortable and supportive.

3. **Downsize with Intention**
   Moving into a smaller space means you'll need to be selective about what you bring with you. Focus on the items that are most meaningful and practical. Many communities have guidelines about what you can bring, so be sure to ask for specifics. Consider donating or gifting items you won't need—this can be a rewarding way to pass on cherished belongings to loved ones or to those in need. Think about what will make your new space feel like home, and prioritize those items.

4. **Personalize Your New Space**
   Just because you're moving into a smaller space doesn't mean it can't feel like home. Bring along photos, artwork, and other items that make you happy. These personal touches can help you feel more comfortable and settled. Arrange your furniture in a way that feels familiar and comforting. Adding your favorite blankets, pillows, and decor can make a big difference. Your new space should reflect your personality and style—it's a fresh start, but it's still your home.

5. **Embrace the Community**
   One of the biggest benefits of assisted living is the opportunity to connect with others. Attend

activities, join clubs, and introduce yourself to your neighbors. Building relationships can help you feel more at home and less isolated. It might feel a bit intimidating at first, but remember that many others are in the same boat, looking to make new friends and connections. Participating in community events can also help you establish a routine and feel more engaged in your new environment.

6. **Stay Connected with Family and Friends**
   While building new relationships is important, staying connected with your existing network of family and friends is equally vital. Schedule regular phone calls, video chats, or visits to maintain those bonds. Sharing your experiences and updates with loved ones can help ease the transition and provide a sense of continuity. You can even invite them to participate in community events or activities, making them a part of your new chapter.

7. **Focus on Your Well-being**
   Assisted living communities often provide resources and support for maintaining your health and well-being. Take advantage of wellness programs, fitness classes, and healthcare services available to you. Staying active and prioritizing your health can enhance your overall quality of life and help you feel more confident and independent.

Remember, this transition is about creating a new chapter that's filled with support, connection, and peace of mind. It's not about giving up independence—it's about embracing a lifestyle that allows you to thrive. By focusing on the positives and taking proactive steps to settle in, you can make this move a fulfilling and rewarding experience. This is your opportunity to explore new interests, form meaningful relationships, and enjoy a vibrant and supportive community. Embrace this new adventure with an open heart and mind—the best is yet to come.

Downsizing While Moving in with Family

Moving in with family is another common downsizing scenario, and it comes with its own set of challenges and rewards. On one hand, it's an opportunity to strengthen family bonds and share daily life with loved ones. On the other hand, it can feel like a loss of independence or a shift in family dynamics.

If you're considering this option, it's important to approach it with open communication and realistic expectations. Here's how to make the transition as smooth as possible:

1. **Have Honest Conversations**
   Before making the move, sit down with your family and discuss everyone's expectations. Talk about things like household responsibilities, privacy, and finances. The more you can address potential issues upfront, the better. It's also helpful to talk about long-term expectations—is this a temporary arrangement, or are you planning to stay indefinitely? Clarifying these details early can help prevent misunderstandings down the road.

2. **Create Your Own Space**
   Even if you're moving into a smaller space within someone else's home, it's important to have a place that feels like your own. Whether it's a bedroom, a corner of the living room, or a cozy nook, make it your sanctuary. Personalize it with familiar items, photos, and decor that make you feel at home. Having a space that reflects your personality can provide comfort and help you adjust to the new environment.

3. **Set Boundaries**
   Living with family can be wonderful, but it's also important to maintain boundaries. Talk about how you'll respect each other's privacy and independence. For example, you might agree on certain times when you'll have the house to yourself or establish routines that give everyone some alone time. Boundaries aren't just about physical space—they also apply to emotional and social aspects. Discuss how to handle conflicts or sensitive topics, and make sure everyone feels heard and respected.

4. **Stay Connected to Your Own Life**
   Just because you're living with family doesn't mean you have to give up your own interests and routines. Stay involved in hobbies, clubs, and social activities that bring you joy. This will help you maintain a sense of independence and fulfillment. Consider volunteering, joining local community groups, or taking classes to meet new people and stay engaged. Maintaining your own

social circle can provide balance and prevent feelings of isolation.

5. **Be Flexible**
   Living with family is a big adjustment for everyone involved, and it's normal to have some bumps along the way. Be willing to adapt and compromise as you settle into your new living arrangement. Flexibility is key—whether it's adjusting to new household routines, sharing common spaces, or navigating differing lifestyles. Remember, patience and understanding go a long way in creating a harmonious living environment.

6. **Contribute to the Household**
   Contributing to the household can foster a sense of belonging and mutual respect. This doesn't just mean financially—although discussing shared expenses is important—but also participating in chores, cooking meals, or offering help where needed. Being an active member of the household shows appreciation and helps maintain a balanced dynamic.

7. **Keep the Lines of Communication Open**
   Even after you've settled in, it's important to regularly check in with your family about how things are going. Open communication helps address any issues early before they become bigger problems. Schedule regular family meetings or casual check-ins to discuss any concerns, share feedback, and celebrate the positives of living together.

Moving in with family can be a beautiful way to strengthen relationships and create a sense of togetherness. With open communication and a spirit of cooperation, it can be a rewarding experience for everyone involved. By approaching the move thoughtfully and with mutual respect, you can create a living arrangement that benefits both you and your family, fostering deeper connections and shared memories.

Long-Distance Moves and Navigating Out-of-State Transitions

Moving to a new state—or even a new country—is a big adventure, but it can also feel daunting. You're not just leaving behind a home; you're leaving behind a community, a network of friends, and a familiar way of life. Whether you're relocating for a job, family, or simply a change of scenery, the process can be overwhelming without the right preparation and mindset. However, with careful planning and a positive attitude, you can make your long-distance move a smooth and even exciting transition.

If you're facing a long-distance move, here are some tips to help you navigate the transition:

1. **Research Your New Area** Before you move, take the time to learn about your new community. What's the climate like? Understanding the weather can help you pack appropriately and prepare for any seasonal changes. For example, if you're moving from a warm climate to a colder one, you'll need to invest in winter gear you might not currently own. What are the local amenities? Look into grocery stores, healthcare facilities, schools, and recreational areas. Knowing where to find essential services will make settling in much easier.

Additionally, find out if there are clubs or organizations that align with your interests. Whether it's a local book club, a hiking group, or a community theater, engaging in activities you enjoy can help you meet like-minded people and feel more connected to your new home. The more you know about your new area, the more prepared you'll feel, and the quicker you'll adapt.

2. **Plan a Visit** If possible, visit your new area before the move. This will give you a chance to explore neighborhoods, check out housing options, and get a feel for the community. Walking the streets, visiting local shops, and dining at nearby restaurants can provide valuable insights that online research simply can't offer. You might discover hidden gems or decide that a different neighborhood suits your lifestyle better.

A pre-move visit can also help ease some of the anxiety about the unknown. Seeing your future home and surroundings in person can make the move feel more real and less intimidating. Take notes, snap photos, and create a list of places you want to explore further once you're settled in.

3. **Stay Connected to Your Old Community** Just because you're moving doesn't mean you have to lose touch with the people and places you love. Schedule regular phone calls or video chats with friends and family to maintain those important relationships. Social media can also be a great tool for staying in touch and sharing updates about your new life.

Consider planning visits back to your old community when possible. Having a trip to look forward to can help ease feelings of homesickness. Additionally, inviting friends and family to visit you in your new home can help them understand your new environment and create new memories together.

4. **Build a New Support Network** One of the hardest parts of a long-distance move is leaving behind your support system. But with time and effort, you can build a new one. Start by introducing yourself to your neighbors—a simple hello can go a long way in establishing friendly connections. Attend local events, whether it's a farmers' market, a community festival, or a town hall meeting. These gatherings provide excellent opportunities to meet people and learn more about your new community.

Joining local groups or clubs can also be incredibly helpful. Whether it's a fitness class, a hobby group, or a volunteer organization, participating in group activities can help you meet new people and build meaningful connections. Don't be afraid to put yourself out there—building a support network takes time, but it's well worth the effort.

5. **Embrace the Adventure** Moving to a new place is an opportunity to start fresh and try new things. Approach your move with an open mind and a sense of curiosity. Explore your new area—visit local landmarks, try new restaurants, and immerse yourself in the local culture. Taking up a new hobby or learning a new skill can also be a great way to embrace your new environment. Whether it's learning to cook a regional dish, picking up a

new sport, or taking a local history class, engaging in new activities can make your new home feel exciting and vibrant.

Volunteering for a cause you care about is another excellent way to integrate into your new community. It not only allows you to give back but also connects you with people who share your values and interests. The more you embrace the adventure, the more you'll feel at home in your new community.

Additional Tips for a Smooth Transition

- **Organize Your Move Efficiently:** Make a detailed moving checklist and timeline to keep track of tasks like hiring movers, packing, and notifying important contacts of your address change. Label your boxes clearly, and consider creating an "essentials" box with items you'll need immediately upon arrival, like toiletries, basic kitchen supplies, and important documents.

- **Manage Your Finances:** Moving long-distance can be expensive, so it's essential to budget carefully. Factor in costs like transportation, temporary housing, and utility deposits. Keep track of receipts—some moving expenses may be tax-deductible, especially if the move is job-related.

- **Take Care of Legal and Administrative Tasks:** Update your address with the postal service, banks, and insurance providers. If you're moving to a new state, you may need to get a new driver's license, register your vehicle, and update your voter registration. Make sure to transfer medical records and prescriptions to healthcare providers in your new area.

- **Give Yourself Time to Adjust:** It's normal to feel a mix of excitement and homesickness after a big move. Allow yourself time to settle in and adapt to your new surroundings. Be patient with yourself as you navigate this transition, and don't hesitate to seek support if you're feeling overwhelmed.

In conclusion, while long-distance moves come with their share of challenges, they also offer incredible opportunities for growth and new experiences. With thorough research, thoughtful planning, and a willingness to embrace change, you can turn your move into an exciting new chapter in your life. Remember, every new place has something unique to offer—all it takes is an open heart and a curious spirit to find it.

Final Thoughts: Finding Joy in the Journey

No matter what your downsizing scenario looks like, remember that this is a journey—one that's filled with challenges, yes, but also opportunities for growth, connection, and joy. Downsizing isn't just about letting go of things; it's about making space for what truly matters. Whether you're moving to a smaller home, decluttering years of accumulated belongings, or simplifying your lifestyle, every step you take brings you closer to a life that reflects your current needs and future aspirations.

So, as you navigate this transition, be kind to yourself. Downsizing can be emotionally and physically taxing, but it's also incredibly rewarding. Celebrate the small victories—whether it's clearing out a single drawer or finally deciding what to do with that box of old photos. Each accomplishment, no matter how minor it seems, is a step forward. Lean on your support system, whether it's friends, family, or professional organizers. Sharing the journey with others can provide comfort, encouragement, and even a few laughs along the way.

Take things one step at a time. It's easy to feel overwhelmed when faced with a house full of belongings, but breaking the process into manageable tasks can make it feel more achievable. Set realistic goals, and don't be afraid to take breaks when needed. Remember, this isn't a race—it's a personal journey, and it's important to move at a pace that feels right for you.

And most importantly, remember that you're not just downsizing—you're creating a new chapter that's filled with possibility and promise. This is your chance to redefine what home means to you, to curate a living space that brings you joy and peace. Imagine the freedom that comes with having less clutter and more clarity, the opportunities that arise from simplifying your surroundings. Downsizing can open doors to new experiences, relationships, and adventures that you might not have considered before.

May this journey lead you to a life that's lighter, more intentional, and filled with joy. Cheers to embracing change, to finding beauty in simplicity, and to discovering the endless possibilities that await you in this new chapter of your life!

Chapter 10: Downsizing Without Moving

Let's talk about something that doesn't get enough attention: downsizing without moving. Yes, you read that right. Downsizing doesn't always mean packing up and relocating to a new home. For many of us, the best option is to stay right where we are—but with a fresh, simplified approach to how we live in our current space. Maybe you love your home and the memories it holds. Maybe you're deeply connected to your community and don't want to leave. Or maybe the idea of moving feels overwhelming, and you'd rather focus on making your current home more manageable and comfortable. Whatever your reasons, downsizing without moving is a valid and often rewarding choice.

So, what does it mean to downsize without moving? At its core, it's about reducing clutter, rethinking how you use your space, and making your home work better for your current lifestyle. It's about letting go of items that no longer serve a purpose and creating an environment that feels open, organized, and easy to maintain.

Start by evaluating each room in your home. Ask yourself: Do I use everything in this space? Are there items that I haven't touched in years? Are there areas that feel crowded or overwhelming? This process isn't about getting rid of everything, but rather about being intentional with what you keep.

One effective strategy is the "one room at a time" approach. Instead of trying to tackle your entire home at once, focus on one room or area. This makes the process feel more manageable and less daunting. Start with a space that you use frequently, like the kitchen or living room, and work your way through the house.

As you go through your belongings, consider the "joy" factor. Does this item bring you joy or serve a practical purpose? If not, it might be time to let it go. You can donate items to charity, give them to family or friends, or even sell them if they're in good condition. The goal is to create a living space that feels light, functional, and reflective of your current needs.

Furniture is another area where downsizing can make a big impact. Do you have large, bulky pieces that take up too much space? Consider replacing them with smaller, more versatile furniture. For example, a large dining table that seats ten might be swapped for a smaller, extendable table that better fits your current lifestyle. Multi-functional furniture, like ottomans with storage or fold-out couches, can also help maximize space.

Storage solutions play a key role in downsizing without moving. Look for creative ways to organize your belongings, such as under-bed storage, wall-mounted shelves, or closet organizers. The idea is to make the most of your available space while keeping everything neat and accessible.

Another important aspect of downsizing without moving is making your home more comfortable and safe, especially if you plan to age in place. This might include installing grab bars in the bathroom, adding better lighting to reduce the risk of falls, or rearranging furniture to create wider, more accessible pathways. Think about how your needs might change over time and make adjustments that will support your comfort and independence.

Simplifying your home can also have a positive impact on your mental well-being. A clutter-free environment can reduce stress, increase your sense of control, and make your daily routines more enjoyable. It's amazing how much lighter and freer you can feel when you're not surrounded by excess stuff.

Of course, downsizing without moving isn't just about the physical space—it's also about shifting your mindset. Embrace the idea that less can be more. Focus on the things that truly matter to you, whether it's spending time with loved ones, pursuing hobbies, or simply enjoying a peaceful, organized home.

In addition to the practical benefits, downsizing without moving can also lead to financial savings. By reducing clutter and optimizing your home, you might find that you need less maintenance, lower utility bills, and fewer expenses overall. This can free up resources for other things you enjoy, like travel, hobbies, or spoiling your grandkids.

It's also worth considering how your simplified home might affect your future plans. If you ever decide to move, having a decluttered, well-organized home can make the process much easier and less stressful. Plus, a tidy home is often more appealing to potential buyers if you ever choose to sell.

Finally, remember that downsizing without moving is a personal journey. There's no one-size-fits-all approach, and it's important to go at your own pace. Celebrate your progress, no matter how small, and recognize the positive changes you're making in your life.

In this chapter, we've explored how to simplify your current home for easier living, embrace the "aging in place" approach, and decide when staying put is the best option for you. Downsizing without moving is about creating a home that supports your lifestyle, brings you joy, and makes everyday life a little bit easier.

So, grab your coffee (or tea), and let's dive into the practical steps you can take to start downsizing right where you are. It's time to make your home a place that feels just right—not too big, not too cluttered, but perfectly suited to the life you want to live.

Simplifying Your Current Home for Easier Living

Let's start with something simple but transformative: simplifying your home. Even if you're not planning to move anytime soon, decluttering and reorganizing your living space can have a surprisingly big impact on how your home feels and functions. It's not just about tidying up—it's about creating an environment that supports the life you want to live, rather than one that feels heavy or overwhelming.

Here's the thing: over the years, it's incredibly easy for our homes to accumulate stuff. We all do it. From old gadgets we thought we'd use, to clothes that no longer fit, to gifts we've held onto out of guilt, our homes slowly fill with items that may no longer serve a purpose. Some of this stuff we've forgotten about entirely, and some of it we keep "just in case." But all those things—no matter how small—can pile up and start to affect the way we live. A cluttered home can make it harder to move around freely, harder to clean efficiently, and even harder to relax and enjoy your space. Simplifying your home isn't just about aesthetics; it's about reclaiming your space and making it work better for *you.*

So, where do you begin?

It might feel like a big task, but breaking it down into smaller steps can make the process manageable—and even enjoyable. Here are some practical tips to get you started on the path to a simpler, more functional home.

1. Tackle One Room at a Time

Trying to declutter your entire house in one go is a recipe for frustration. It can quickly feel overwhelming, especially if you've lived in the same place for many years. Instead, focus on one room at a time—or even just one corner of a room. Start with the spaces that feel the most cluttered or stressful. The kitchen, for example, is often a hotspot for unused gadgets and mismatched containers. Or maybe it's the garage, overflowing with tools and boxes of who-knows-what. The spare bedroom is another common catch-all for things we don't know what to do with. By zeroing in on one area, you can make noticeable progress without feeling like the task is impossible.

2. Ask Yourself the Right Questions

As you go through your belongings, it's important to be honest with yourself. Ask questions like: *Do I use this? Do I love this? Does this add value to my life?* If the answer to any of these is no, it might be time to let it go. And that's okay! Remember, simplifying your home isn't about getting rid of everything you own—it's about keeping what matters. Sentimental items are fine to keep, even if they don't serve a practical purpose, as long as they genuinely bring you joy. But if you're holding onto something out of obligation or habit, it might be time to say goodbye.

3. Create Zones for Different Activities

One of the secrets to simplifying your home is to create clear, functional zones for different activities. Think about how you use your space: is there a specific area where you like to read? A spot where you do hobbies or crafts? A place where you unwind at the end of the day? By designating certain areas for specific activities, you can make the most of your space and reduce the likelihood of clutter creeping in. For example, having a dedicated reading nook with a comfy chair and a small shelf for books can help keep your living room tidy and organized.

4. Invest in Smart Storage Solutions

Storage is your best friend when it comes to simplifying your home. But it's not just about stuffing things out of sight—it's about finding storage solutions that are both functional and visually pleasing. Look for baskets, bins, shelves, and other organizers that fit your style and your needs. Clear storage containers can be helpful for items you don't use every day but still want to keep track of. The goal is to keep your belongings organized and easy to find, while also maintaining a clean, open feel in your home.

5. Let Go of Guilt

This might be the hardest part of the process: letting go of items that have sentimental value or that you feel guilty about discarding. Maybe it's a gift from a loved one, or something you spent a lot of money on but never use. But here's the truth: holding onto something out of guilt doesn't honor the item—or the person who gave it to you. It just adds unnecessary weight to your life. Instead, focus on keeping the things that truly bring you joy, and let the rest go with gratitude. You can even donate items so they find a new home where they'll be appreciated.

Simplifying your home isn't just about getting rid of stuff—it's about creating a space that feels calm, comfortable, and aligned with your current needs and lifestyle. And the best part? You don't have to do it all at once. Take your time, go at your own pace, and enjoy the process. Every small step you take brings you closer to a home that feels lighter, more organized, and easier to live in. And that's a change worth making.

The "Aging in Place" Approach

Now, let's talk about aging in place. This is a term you've probably heard before, but what does it really mean? At its core, aging in place is about staying in your own home as you grow older, rather than moving to a retirement community or assisted living facility. It's about maintaining your independence and continuing to live in a place that feels familiar and comfortable.

For many of us, aging in place is the ideal scenario. It allows us to stay connected to our neighborhoods, routines, and the memories we've built over the years. But while it's an appealing option, it does require some planning and preparation to ensure safety, comfort, and overall well-being. Here's how to make it work:

1. **Make Your Home Safe and Accessible**
   As we age, our physical needs change, and our homes need to adapt alongside us. Start by identifying potential hazards, like loose rugs that could cause trips, poor lighting that makes it hard to see at night, or steep stairs that become difficult to navigate. Simple modifications like installing grab bars in the bathroom, adding ramps or stairlifts, and widening doorways for a wheelchair or walker can make a huge difference. Even switching out doorknobs for lever handles can help if arthritis becomes an issue.

2. **Focus on Single-Level Living**
   If your home has multiple levels, consider creating a single-level living space. This might mean moving your bedroom to the main floor or adding a bathroom on the ground level. The goal is to reduce the need to navigate stairs, which can become more challenging as you age. If moving isn't possible, installing a stairlift or even a residential elevator might be worth considering.

3. **Embrace Smart Technology**
   Technology can be a game-changer when it comes to aging in place. Smart home devices like voice-activated assistants allow you to control lights, adjust the thermostat, or even lock doors without moving from your chair. Medical alert systems offer peace of mind by providing immediate access to emergency help if needed. Video doorbells let you see who's at the door without getting up, and automated pill dispensers can help you stay on track with medications.

4. **Build a Support Network**
   Aging in place doesn't mean doing everything on your own. It's important to build a network of support, whether it's family, friends, neighbors, or professional caregivers. This network can help with tasks like grocery shopping, home maintenance, or transportation to appointments. Local community centers often offer senior programs, and many neighborhoods have volunteer organizations that assist with everyday needs.

5. **Plan for the Future**
   Finally, it's crucial to think ahead. What will you do if your health needs change or you face an unexpected emergency? Consider having a financial plan for potential home modifications or healthcare expenses. Establish a healthcare directive, and keep emergency contact information easily accessible. It's also wise to discuss long-term care options with your family, even if you hope to stay in your home indefinitely.

Aging in place is about more than just staying in your home—it's about creating a lifestyle that allows you to thrive as you grow older. With the right preparation and support, it can be a fulfilling and empowering choice that lets you maintain independence and enjoy your golden years in the comfort of your own space.

Final Thoughts: Finding Joy in the Home You Have

Downsizing without moving isn't just about clearing out closets or rearranging furniture—it's about reimagining your space in a way that nurtures your well-being and supports the life you want to live today. It's about creating a home that not only functions better but also feels better. Your home should be a place that brings you joy, reflects your values, and provides a sense of peace and comfort. It's about honoring the memories and treasures of the past while making room for new experiences and opportunities in the present and future.

As you go through this journey—whether you're simplifying your space to reduce stress, making thoughtful modifications to age gracefully in place, or choosing to stay put because of the deep emotional connection you have to your home—remember that this process is deeply personal. There's no one-size-fits-all approach, no perfect way to do it. The important thing is to listen to yourself, respect your own pace, and create an environment that feels like a true reflection of who you are today.

Maybe that means letting go of items that no longer serve a purpose, or maybe it means repurposing old pieces in new ways. It might involve redesigning a room to make it more accessible, or simply finding new joy in a familiar corner of your home. Whatever your path, know that it's valid and meaningful. You're crafting a space that aligns with your current lifestyle, needs, and dreams, and that's something to be proud of.

So, take a deep breath and savor the process. It's not just about the physical changes—it's about the emotional and mental clarity that comes from creating a space that truly feels like *you.* Your home is more than just four walls and a roof; it's your sanctuary, your safe haven, and a canvas for the life you're living. With a little effort and intention, you can transform it into exactly what you need for this next exciting chapter.

Here's to finding joy in the home you have—to embracing the beauty in simplicity, the peace in letting go, and the excitement of new beginnings without ever leaving the place you love. May your home be filled with warmth, purpose, and endless possibilities.

Cheers to a life well-lived, right where you are!

Chapter 11: Leaving a Legacy

Let's talk about something that's on many of our minds as we age: leaving a legacy. It's not just about the stuff we leave behind—it's about the stories, the memories, and the values that we pass on to future generations. Whether it's a cherished family heirloom, a box of old photos, or a lifetime of wisdom, we all want to leave something meaningful behind.

But here's the thing: leaving a legacy isn't just about what we leave—it's about how we leave it. It's about making sure that our treasures are passed on in a way that's thoughtful, intentional, and, most importantly, not burdensome to those who come after us.

When we think about leaving physical items like heirlooms, it's easy to assume that our loved ones will know what's important and why. But without context, even the most cherished possessions can lose their meaning. That's why it's so important to share the stories behind these items. Maybe it's your grandmother's quilt that kept you warm on cold nights, or your father's watch that he wore every day for thirty years. Telling these stories not only preserves the item's significance but also connects future generations to their roots.

Consider creating a legacy journal or recording audio or video stories about these items. It doesn't have to be fancy—just a simple explanation of why an object matters to you can make all the difference. You'd be surprised how a small story can transform an ordinary item into a priceless treasure.

But leaving a legacy goes beyond physical items. Think about the values and lessons you want to pass down. Maybe it's your work ethic, your love for nature, or your commitment to kindness. These intangible gifts often have the most lasting impact. Consider writing letters to your loved ones, sharing your hopes and dreams for them, or even creating a family mission statement that reflects the principles you hold dear.

Now, let's talk about the digital world—because let's face it, we're living in an age where much of our lives are stored online. Photos, emails, social media accounts… it can be overwhelming to think about how to manage all this digital clutter. But digital downsizing is just as important as sorting through physical possessions.

Start by organizing your digital photos and documents. Create folders for different events or periods in your life, and delete duplicates or irrelevant files. Consider using cloud storage to keep everything safe and accessible to those you trust. And don't forget to leave instructions for accessing these digital memories—passwords, account information, and any other details that might be needed.

Another aspect of digital legacy is deciding what happens to your online presence after you're gone. Many social media platforms offer options for memorializing accounts or assigning a legacy contact who can manage your profile. Taking the time to set this up can prevent confusion and help your loved ones preserve your digital memory in a way that feels right to them.

Of course, planning for the future isn't just about stuff—it's also about ensuring your wishes are respected and your loved ones are cared for. This means having important conversations about your estate plan, your healthcare preferences, and your final wishes. It might feel uncomfortable, but these discussions can relieve a lot of stress for your family down the road.

Consider working with an estate planner to create a will or trust that clearly outlines how your assets should be distributed. This can help prevent disputes and ensure that your legacy is preserved according to your wishes. Don't forget to update these documents regularly, especially after major life events like births, deaths, or changes in your financial situation.

You might also want to think about charitable giving as part of your legacy. Donating to causes you care about can be a powerful way to make a lasting impact. Whether it's setting up a scholarship fund, contributing to a favorite charity, or supporting community projects, your generosity can continue to make a difference long after you're gone.

Finally, remember that leaving a legacy isn't a one-time event—it's an ongoing process. It's about living your life in a way that reflects your values and priorities. The relationships you build, the kindness you show, and the lessons you teach every day are all part of the legacy you leave behind.

In this chapter, we've explored how to ensure your heirlooms and stories live on, how to tackle the often-overwhelming task of digital downsizing, and how to plan for future generations without overwhelming them. By taking thoughtful, intentional steps, you can leave a legacy that's meaningful, lasting, and truly reflective of the life you've lived.

At the end of the day, the most valuable legacy isn't the things we leave behind—it's the love, memories, and values that continue to live on in the hearts of those we've touched.

Ensuring Your Heirlooms and Stories Live On

Let's start with the tangible stuff—the heirlooms, the keepsakes, the items that hold so much meaning for you and your family. Maybe it's your grandmother's wedding ring, your father's pocket watch, or the quilt your mother made by hand. These items are more than just objects—they're pieces of your family's history, carrying with them the weight of memories, traditions, and the people who came before you.

But here's the challenge: not everyone values these items in the same way. What's precious to you might not hold the same significance for your children or grandchildren. And that's okay. Every generation sees the world through a different lens, and while some might treasure the past, others may prioritize the present or future. The key is to pass these items on in a way that honors their meaning while respecting the preferences of the next generation. Here's how to do it:

1. **Have the Conversation**
   Start by talking to your family about the items you want to pass on. This isn't just about deciding who gets what—it's about opening up a dialogue about your family's history and values. Share why certain items are important to you and listen to what your family members have to say. Ask them what they're interested in and what they'd like to keep. You might be surprised by what resonates with them. Maybe your granddaughter has always admired that old locket you wore, or your son has

fond memories of the fishing rod you used on family trips. These conversations can be a meaningful way to connect and ensure that your cherished items go to someone who will truly appreciate them.

2. **Document the Stories**
   The value of an heirloom often lies in the story behind it. A necklace is just a necklace—until you know it was given to your grandmother on her wedding day. A simple kitchen spoon becomes priceless when you learn it stirred the pot of soup your great-grandmother made during tough times. Take the time to write down or record the history of these items. Who did they belong to? What's their significance? What memories do they hold? You can create a family heirloom journal, or even record short videos explaining the stories behind each item. These stories can be just as meaningful as the items themselves, providing a rich tapestry of your family's past that can be passed down alongside the physical objects.

3. **Consider a Family Heirloom Day**
   If you have a lot of items to pass on, consider hosting a family heirloom day. This can be a special event where your family gathers to celebrate your shared history. Lay out the items, share the stories behind each one, and let your family choose what they'd like to take. This can be a beautiful way to connect, reminisce, and ensure that your treasures find a new home where they'll be cherished. It's also a wonderful

opportunity to see your family's reactions and hear their own memories connected to these items. Sometimes, an object you didn't think much of can hold deep significance for someone else.

4. **Be Open to Letting Go**
   Not every heirloom will find a new home within your family, and that's okay. It's important to recognize that the emotional attachment you have to an item might not be shared by others. If an item doesn't hold meaning for anyone in your family, consider donating it to a museum, historical society, or charity. This way, it can still be appreciated and cherished, even if it's not by your own family. Some items might have historical or cultural value that extends beyond your family, and sharing them with the broader community can be a way of honoring their significance.

Remember, the goal isn't to pass on every single item—it's to pass on the ones that truly matter, along with the stories and values that make them meaningful. By thoughtfully selecting which heirlooms to keep, documenting their stories, and engaging your family in the process, you ensure that your family's history lives on in a way that's both respectful and meaningful. The objects may change hands, but the love, memories, and lessons they carry will continue to inspire and connect future generations.

Digital Downsizing: Managing Photos and Documents

In today's world, digital clutter has quietly become as overwhelming as physical clutter. From thousands of photos stored across devices to countless emails and documents scattered in various folders, our digital lives can become chaotic without us even realizing it. If left unchecked, this digital mess could become a burden for our loved ones to handle later on. But with a little time and effort, you can simplify your digital life and ensure your digital legacy is both meaningful and manageable.

1. Start with Photos

If you're like most people, your phone, computer, and cloud storage are bursting with photos—some meaningful, many duplicates, and others blurry or accidental. Tackling your photo collection might seem daunting, but it's one of the most rewarding parts of digital downsizing.

- **Delete the Unnecessary:** Begin by deleting photos that are blurry, duplicates, or don't hold any sentimental value.

- **Organize Thoughtfully:** Once you've trimmed the excess, organize the remaining photos into folders by year, event, or theme. This makes it easier to find special moments and relive cherished memories.

- **Use Photo Management Tools:** Consider using photo organization apps that can help you tag, sort, and even enhance your pictures.

2. Back Up Your Files

After you've organized your photos and documents, the next crucial step is ensuring they are safely backed up. Digital files are vulnerable to loss through hardware failure, accidental deletion, or even cyber threats.

- **External Hard Drives:** Invest in a reliable external hard drive to keep a physical backup of your files.

- **Cloud Storage Services:** Use trusted cloud services like Google Drive, Dropbox, or iCloud to store your files securely online. Many of these services offer automatic backup features, saving you time and effort.

- **Double Backup Strategy:** For extra security, consider using both an external hard drive and a cloud service. This redundancy ensures that even if one method fails, your files are still protected.

3. Share Your Digital Legacy

Your digital collection isn't just for you—it's a treasure trove of memories and important documents that your family will cherish. Creating a digital archive is a thoughtful way to pass down your legacy.

- **Create a Digital Archive:** Compile your favorite photos, home videos, important documents, and even cherished recipes or playlists.

- **Use Family-Friendly Platforms:** Platforms like Google Photos, Apple Shared Albums, or specialized legacy services make it easy to organize and share your digital archive.

- **Write Contextual Notes:** Add descriptions or stories to your photos and videos, providing context that your loved ones will appreciate.

4. Simplify Your Online Presence

Over the years, you may have accumulated numerous online accounts—some active, others long forgotten. Simplifying your online presence ensures your digital footprint is easy to manage.

- **Review and Delete Accounts:** Identify accounts you no longer use and delete them. This includes old social media profiles, unused email addresses, and outdated subscriptions.

- **Document Important Accounts:** Make a list of essential accounts, such as email, social media, online banking, and investment platforms. Ensure your loved ones know how to access these if needed.

- **Update Security Settings:** Regularly update passwords and enable two-factor authentication for your important accounts to keep them secure.

5. Consider a Digital Executor

Just as you might appoint someone to manage your estate, it's wise to designate a digital executor—a trusted person who will handle your digital assets after you're gone.

- **Choose the Right Person:** Select someone tech-savvy and trustworthy who understands your wishes.

- **Provide Clear Instructions:** Document your preferences for managing your digital files, closing accounts, or even creating online memorials.
- **Legal Considerations:** Check if your state allows for the legal appointment of a digital executor, and include this role in your will or estate plan if possible.

The Importance of Digital Downsizing

While sorting through physical belongings can be an emotional journey, digital downsizing offers a unique opportunity to curate your digital legacy thoughtfully. It ensures that your most treasured memories, important documents, and online presence are preserved in a way that's manageable for your loved ones.

By taking these steps now, you not only declutter your digital life but also provide a lasting gift to your family—a well-organized, meaningful digital archive that tells your story in the most thoughtful way possible.

Planning for Future Generations Without Burdening Them

Finally, let's talk about the bigger picture: planning for future generations in a way that's thoughtful and considerate. It's natural to want to leave something behind for your children, grandchildren, and even great-grandchildren. But it's also important to make sure that your legacy is a gift, not a burden.

Here's how to do it:

1. Be Clear About Your Wishes One of the best ways to avoid burdening your loved ones is to be clear about your wishes. This includes everything from your will and estate plan to your preferences for end-of-life care. Make sure your documents are up to date, and communicate your wishes to

your family. When everyone understands your intentions, it reduces the likelihood of disputes or confusion later on. Regularly revisiting these plans ensures they reflect your current desires and circumstances. It's also wise to appoint a trusted executor or power of attorney to carry out your plans, ensuring your wishes are respected and followed.

2. Simplify Your Estate If your estate is complex, consider simplifying it. This might mean consolidating accounts, reducing the number of beneficiaries, or creating a trust. The simpler your estate, the easier it will be for your loved ones to manage. Trusts can also help avoid probate, saving time and legal expenses for your heirs. Simplifying doesn't mean you have to sacrifice your financial goals—it means making thoughtful choices that align with both your needs and the future responsibilities of your family. Additionally, consider digital assets, such as online accounts and cryptocurrencies, and include instructions for managing them.

3. Leave a Letter or Video In addition to your legal documents, consider leaving a personal letter or video for your family. This can be a beautiful way to share your thoughts, values, and wishes, and to provide comfort and guidance after you're gone. A heartfelt message can offer clarity and peace, serving as a reminder of your love and the life lessons you hope to pass on. These personal touches can be more impactful than any financial

inheritance, as they capture your essence and the unique bond you shared with each family member. Take time to express gratitude, share stories, and leave behind a piece of your heart.

4. Think About the Emotional Legacy Your legacy isn't just about the stuff you leave behind—it's about the impact you've had on the people around you. Take the time to nurture your relationships, share your wisdom, and create memories with your loved ones. These are the things that will truly live on. Consider documenting family traditions, recipes, or stories that can be passed down through generations. The values you instill—such as kindness, resilience, and integrity—will shape how your family remembers you and how they carry forward your influence in their lives.

5. Be Mindful of Sentimental Items While it's natural to want to pass on sentimental items, it's important to be mindful of how much you're leaving behind. Too many items can become overwhelming for your loved ones. Focus on the ones that are truly meaningful, and let the rest go with gratitude. You can also involve your family in the process of selecting which items hold the most significance to them. This not only ensures that your treasures are appreciated but also fosters meaningful conversations and connections. Creating a list of the stories behind certain items can add even more value and context to these keepsakes.

6. Financial Planning for Future Generations Another key aspect of planning for future generations is considering how your financial legacy will impact them. While leaving a substantial inheritance can be a generous gesture, it's essential to think about how it will affect your heirs' lives. Providing financial education and guidance can help them manage their inheritance wisely. You might also consider setting up scholarships, charitable donations, or family foundations that reflect your values and support causes you care about. These initiatives can create a lasting positive impact and teach future generations the importance of giving back.

7. Addressing Potential Conflicts Family dynamics can be complex, and inheritance issues can sometimes lead to disputes. To prevent conflicts, have open and honest conversations with your loved ones about your plans. Transparency can help manage expectations and reduce misunderstandings. If necessary, involve a mediator or estate planner to facilitate discussions and ensure everyone feels heard and respected. By addressing potential issues proactively, you can foster harmony and ensure your legacy brings your family closer together.

Planning for future generations is about more than just passing on material possessions—it's about leaving behind a legacy of love, wisdom, and values. By taking the time to plan thoughtfully and intentionally, you can ensure that your legacy is a gift that enriches the lives of those who come after you. The true measure of your legacy lies in the memories you create, the lessons you impart, and the love you leave behind. With careful planning and heartfelt consideration, you can make sure your impact endures for generations to come.

Final Thoughts: Creating a Legacy That Lasts

Leaving a legacy is one of the most meaningful things we can do as we move through life. It's about more than just the *stuff* we leave behind—it's about the stories, the memories, and the values that we pass on to future generations. It's the quiet moments of wisdom you've shared over the years, the laughter around the dinner table, and the lessons you've taught without even realizing it. These are the pieces of your legacy that will echo through time.

As you navigate this process, remember to be kind to yourself. It's not about perfection—it's about *intention.* No one leaves behind a flawless legacy, and that's perfectly okay. Life is messy, unpredictable, and beautifully imperfect. What matters most is the heart you put into the choices you make and the people you touch along the way. Take the time to reflect on what's truly important to you—whether it's family, friendships, or contributions to your community—and focus on the things that will have the most lasting impact on the people you love.

Think of your legacy as more than just a final chapter. It's the entire story of your life, filled with the ups and downs, the triumphs and the lessons learned. And every day, you're adding to that story. The way you show kindness to a stranger, the support you give to a friend in need, the patience you extend in difficult moments—all of these things matter. They become part of the tapestry of your life, woven into the memories and hearts of those you leave behind.

And most importantly, remember that your legacy isn't just about what you leave behind—it's about the life you've *lived* and the love you've *shared.* It's about showing up, being present, and embracing the people and experiences that make your life rich and meaningful. So, take a deep breath, and enjoy the journey. Your legacy is already being written, one day at a time, in the smiles you inspire, the lessons you teach, and the love you give freely.

As you move forward, think about the little things that can make a big difference. Maybe it's writing a letter to your grandchildren, sharing stories of your life and the wisdom you've gained. Maybe it's volunteering your time to a cause you believe in, or mentoring someone who could benefit from your experience. Even the smallest actions can leave the deepest impressions.

Here's to creating a legacy that lasts, and to leaving behind a world that's a little brighter because of the love and wisdom you've shared. May your journey be filled with purpose, joy, and connection, and may those you leave behind carry your spirit forward with pride and gratitude.

Conclusion: Celebrating Your New, Simplified Life

Well, here we are—the end of our journey together. If you've made it this far, chances are you've already taken some big steps toward decluttering, downsizing, and creating a simpler, more intentional life. Or maybe you're just starting to dip your toes into the idea. Either way, I want to take a moment to celebrate you. This isn't an easy process, and the fact that you're even considering it—or actively working through it—is a huge accomplishment. Downsizing isn't just about getting rid of stuff or moving to a smaller space. It's about making room—for new experiences, new relationships, and new possibilities. It's about letting go of what no longer serves you so you can embrace what truly matters. It bears repeating, another emotional hurdle is the guilt that can come with downsizing.

So, let's take a moment to reflect on where you've been, where you're going, and how far you've already come. Let's talk about what it means to celebrate your new, simplified life, offer some final words of encouragement, and share a few inspirational stories from retirees who've been where you are and come out the other side feeling lighter, freer, and more fulfilled.

Celebrating Your New, Simplified Life

Let's start with the celebration. Because yes, this is a moment worth celebrating. Downsizing is a big deal. It's not just a physical process—it's an emotional one, too. And when you reach the other side of it, whether you're fully there or still on the journey, it's important to take a moment to acknowledge what you've accomplished.

Think about it: you've taken a hard look at your life and your belongings and made intentional decisions about what to keep and what to let go. You've faced the emotions that come with saying goodbye to a home, a neighborhood, or even just a way of life. You've navigated the logistics of moving, selling, or reorganizing. And through it all, you've shown resilience, courage, and a willingness to embrace change.

That's no small feat.

So, how do you celebrate? It doesn't have to be a big, elaborate party (unless you want it to be!). It can be as simple as taking a moment to sit in your new space and appreciate how it feels. Maybe it's lighter, quieter, or more peaceful. Maybe it's filled with the things you love most, and nothing more. Whatever it is, take a deep breath and let yourself feel proud of what you've created.

You might also celebrate by doing something you've been putting off because you were too busy or too overwhelmed. Maybe it's finally starting that hobby you've always wanted to try, or taking a trip to visit family or friends. Maybe it's just spending a quiet afternoon reading a book or enjoying a cup of tea without the weight of clutter hanging over you.

However you choose to celebrate, make it meaningful. This is your moment to acknowledge the hard work you've done and the new chapter you've opened.

Reflecting on Your Journey

As you settle into this new phase of life, it's helpful to take a step back and reflect on your journey. What lessons have you learned along the way? What surprised you about the process? What challenges did you overcome, and how did you grow from them?

For many, the process of downsizing brings up unexpected emotions. Maybe you found it harder than you thought to let go of certain items. Or perhaps you discovered a sense of freedom you didn't anticipate. Whatever your experience, it's all part of the journey.

Consider keeping a journal of your reflections. Writing down your thoughts and feelings can help you process the experience and gain a deeper understanding of what this transition means for you. Plus, it's a great way to capture memories and milestones that you can look back on in the future.

Reflecting on your journey also means recognizing the people who supported you along the way. Maybe it was family members who helped you pack, friends who offered encouragement, or professionals who guided you through the process. Take a moment to express your gratitude—whether it's a heartfelt thank you, a handwritten note, or a small gesture of appreciation.

Embracing the New Possibilities

Now that you've cleared the physical and emotional clutter, what's next? Downsizing isn't just about what you're leaving behind—it's about what you're moving toward.

Think about the possibilities that lie ahead. Maybe you've freed up time and energy to pursue new interests or hobbies. Perhaps you're excited about meeting new people in your community or spending more time with loved ones. Maybe you're looking forward to traveling, volunteering, or simply enjoying a slower, more intentional pace of life.

Whatever your goals and dreams, now is the time to embrace them. Give yourself permission to explore new opportunities and experiences. Remember, this is your time to create a life that aligns with your values and brings you joy.

Consider setting some intentions or goals for this new chapter. They don't have to be grand or ambitious—even small, simple goals can have a big impact. Maybe it's committing to a daily walk, joining a local club, or learning a new skill. Whatever it is, let it be something that excites and inspires you.

Stories of Inspiration

To inspire you further, here are a few stories from retirees who have embraced the downsizing journey and found fulfillment on the other side.

Mary and John's Story:

Mary and John had lived in their family home for over 40 years. The thought of leaving behind the house where they raised their children was daunting. But as they started the process, they realized how much of their belongings were tied to the past rather than their future. They moved into a smaller condo near the beach, and with less space to maintain, they found more time to travel and visit their grandchildren. "We thought we'd miss the old house," Mary said, "but what we really gained was freedom."

Susan's Story:

After retiring, Susan decided to downsize from her suburban home to a cozy apartment in the city. She was initially worried about the transition, but she soon discovered a vibrant community and a renewed sense of purpose. "I've met so many wonderful people and tried things I never would have before," she shared. "Downsizing wasn't just about the space—it was about finding myself again."

Tom's Story:

Tom had always been a collector, and the idea of parting with his treasures was difficult. But as he started to let go, he realized how much lighter he felt. He donated many of his items to local charities and found joy in knowing they were being appreciated by others. "I thought I'd feel a sense of loss," Tom said, "but what I found was a sense of peace."

Final Words of Encouragement

As we wrap up this journey together, I want to leave you with a few final thoughts.

First, remember that downsizing is a personal journey. There's no right or wrong way to do it, and everyone's path will look a little different. You will never be able to follow every piece of advice in this book and nor should you. Take what you can out of it and make the best of it. Be kind to yourself throughout the process and celebrate every step you take.

Second, keep in mind that this is just the beginning. Downsizing isn't the end of the story—it's the start of a new chapter filled with opportunities and possibilities. Embrace the changes, stay open to new experiences, and trust that you're creating a life that aligns with your values and brings you joy.

Finally, don't forget to celebrate your accomplishments. Whether it's a small moment of reflection or a big, joyful gathering, take the time to acknowledge the hard work you've done and the positive changes you've made. Here's to your new, simplified life—may it be filled with peace, purpose, and endless possibilities.

Final Words of Encouragement

If there's one thing I hope you take away from this book, it's this: you've got this. Downsizing can feel overwhelming at times, but you're stronger and more capable than you think. And you don't have to do it all at once.

Remember, this is your journey. There's no right or wrong way to downsize, and there's no timeline you have to follow. Take it one step at a time, one room at a time, one decision at a time. And if you hit a snag or feel stuck, that's okay. It's all part of the process.

Here are a few final words of encouragement to carry with you:

1. **Be Kind to Yourself**
   Downsizing is emotional. It's okay to feel sad, nostalgic, or even a little lost at times. Give yourself permission to feel those emotions, and don't be too hard on yourself if the process takes longer than you expected.

2. **Focus on the Positives**
   It's easy to get caught up in what you're leaving behind, but try to focus on what you're gaining. A simpler, more manageable home. More time and energy for the things you love. The freedom to live life on your own terms.

3. **Lean on Your Support System**
   You don't have to do this alone. Whether it's family, friends, or a professional organizer, don't be afraid to ask for help. Sometimes, just having someone to talk to can make all the difference.

4. **Trust the Process**
   Downsizing is a journey, and like any journey, it has its ups and downs. Trust that you're moving in the right direction, even if it doesn't always feel that way.

5. **Celebrate the Small Wins**
   Every box you pack, every item you donate, every decision you make is a step forward. Celebrate those small wins along the way—they add up to big changes.

Inspirational Stories from Retirees Who Successfully Downsized

Sometimes, the best encouragement comes from hearing how others have walked this path before us. So, let me share a few stories from retirees who've successfully downsized and come out the other side feeling lighter, freer, and more fulfilled.

Story 1: Mary's Journey to a Cozy Condo

Mary had lived in her four-bedroom family home for over 40 years. It was where she raised her kids, hosted countless family gatherings, and built a lifetime of memories. But after her husband passed away and her kids moved out, the house started to feel too big, too empty, and too much to maintain.

At first, the idea of downsizing felt overwhelming. How could she possibly let go of the home she loved so much? But as she started to go through her belongings, she realized that the memories weren't in the walls or the furniture—they were in her heart.

Mary decided to move to a cozy condo in a nearby retirement community. She brought along her favorite furniture, a few cherished keepsakes, and a whole lot of optimism. And you know what? She's never been happier. She's made new friends, joined a book club, and even started taking painting classes. "I didn't just downsize my home," she says. "I upsized my life."

Story 2: Tom and Linda's Cross-Country Adventure

Tom and Linda had always dreamed of traveling in retirement, but their large family home was holding them back. Between the maintenance, the yard work, and the sheer amount of stuff they'd accumulated over the years, they felt stuck.

One day, they decided enough was enough. They sold their home, donated or sold most of their belongings, and hit the road in an RV. At first, it was a big adjustment. But as they traveled across the country, visiting national parks, meeting new people, and exploring new places, they realized they'd made the right decision.

"We've seen more of the world in the past two years than we did in the previous 20," Tom says. "And the best part? We're living with just the essentials, and it feels amazing."

Story 3: Susan's Simplified Life

Susan had always been a collector. Her home was filled with antiques, books, and memorabilia from her travels. But as she approached retirement, she started to feel weighed down by all her possessions.

She decided to downsize, but instead of moving to a smaller home, she stayed put and simplified her current space. She donated most of her collections, keeping only the items that truly brought her joy. She rearranged her furniture to create a more open, airy feel, and she even turned one of her spare bedrooms into a cozy reading nook.

"I didn't realize how much my stuff was holding me back until I let it go," Susan says. "Now, my home feels like a sanctuary, and I have so much more time and energy for the things I love."

Wrapping It All Up

Downsizing is more than just a practical process—it's a deeply personal journey. It's about letting go of what no longer serves you so you can make room for what truly matters. It's about creating a life that's simpler, more intentional, and more aligned with your values.

As you move forward, remember that this is your journey. There's no right or wrong way to do it, and there's no timeline you have to follow. Take it one step at a time, and don't be afraid to ask for help when you need it.

And most importantly, remember to celebrate along the way. Every decision you make, every item you let go of, every memory you honor is a step toward a simpler, more fulfilling life.

So, here's to you—to your courage, your resilience, and your willingness to embrace change. Here's to the memories you've made, the life you've lived, and the exciting new chapter that's just beginning.

Cheers to your new, simplified life. May it be filled with joy, peace, and endless possibilities.

Appendices

The following appendices are designed to provide you with practical, detailed tools and resources to support you through every stage of the downsizing process. These checklists, templates, and worksheets are tailored to help you stay organized, make informed decisions, and reduce stress. They're not overly simplistic or repetitive—they're actionable and designed to meet the unique needs of seniors navigating this significant life transition.

Appendix A: Checklists, Templates, and Worksheets for Every Stage

1. Pre-Downsizing Assessment Checklist

This checklist helps you evaluate your current situation and determine your downsizing goals.

- **Home Evaluation:**
    - How many rooms do you currently use regularly?
    - Are there areas of your home that feel cluttered or overwhelming?
    - What maintenance tasks are becoming difficult to manage?

- **Lifestyle Goals:**
  - Do you want to travel more in retirement?
  - Are you looking to reduce household chores and maintenance?
  - Do you want to live closer to family or in a more walkable community?
- **Emotional Readiness:**
  - Are you emotionally prepared to let go of belongings or a home with sentimental value?
  - Do you have a support system in place to help you through the process?

2. Room-by-Room Decluttering Worksheet

Use this worksheet to systematically declutter each room in your home.

Room	Items to Keep	Items to Donate/Sell	Items to Discard	Notes
Living Room				
Kitchen				
Bedroom				
Bathroom				
Garage/Storage				

3. Sentimental Items Decision Tree

A flowchart-style template to help you decide what to do with sentimental items:

1. **Does this item bring me joy or hold significant meaning?**
   - Yes → Keep it.
   - No → Move to the next question.
2. **Is this item useful or functional in my daily life?**
   - Yes → Keep it.
   - No → Move to the next question.
3. **Would someone else in my family appreciate this item?**
   - Yes → Offer it to them.
   - No → Consider donating, selling, or discarding.
4. **Can I preserve the memory of this item in another way (e.g., take a photo)?**
   - Yes → Do so, then let the item go.
   - No → Keep it if it's truly irreplaceable.

Appendix B: Sample Moving Timeline and Inventory Sheets

1. Moving Timeline (12-Week Plan)

A detailed timeline to help you stay on track during your move.

Week	Tasks
12 Weeks Before	Research moving companies or services. Begin decluttering room by room.
10 Weeks Before	Schedule estate sale or donation pickups. Start packing non-essential items.
8 Weeks Before	Notify important parties of your move (e.g., banks, insurance, healthcare providers).
6 Weeks Before	Confirm moving date and book movers. Begin packing seasonal items.
4 Weeks Before	Pack up kitchen and other frequently used items. Update your address with the post office.
2 Weeks Before	Confirm details with movers. Pack a "first-night" box with essentials.
Moving Week	Do a final walkthrough of your home. Ensure all utilities are transferred or canceled.

2. Inventory Sheet for Valuables

A template to track and protect your valuables during the move.

Item	Description	Condition	Estimated Value	Packed Location	Notes
Family Heirlooms	Grandmother's ring	Excellent	$1,500	Box 12	Keep with me
Artwork	Oil painting	Good	$800	Box 5	Fragile
Electronics	Laptop	Excellent	$1,200	Personal Bag	Backup data

Appendix C: Financial Planning Templates

1. Downsizing Budget Worksheet

A detailed budget to help you plan for the costs of downsizing.

Category	Estimated Cost	Actual Cost	Notes
Moving Services	$2,000		Get 3 quotes
Home Repairs/Staging	$1,500		Paint touch-ups
New Furniture	$1,000		Sofa, dining table
Storage Unit	$100/month		Short-term
Miscellaneous	$500		Packing supplies

2. Monthly Expense Comparison Worksheet

Compare your current expenses to your projected expenses in your new home.

Expense	Current Home	New Home	Difference
Mortgage/Rent	$1,500	$1,200	-$300
Utilities	$300	$200	-$100
Maintenance	$200	$50	-$150
HOA Fees	$0	$150	+$150
Total	**$2,000**	**$1,600**	**-$400**

Recommended Resources: Websites, Apps, and Professional Services

Websites

- **AARP Downsizing Guide:** Comprehensive tips and resources for seniors.
- **National Association of Senior Move Managers (NASMM):** Find certified professionals to assist with your move.
- **Nextdoor:** Connect with neighbors and local services in your new community.

Apps

- **Sortly:** An inventory app to track your belongings during the move.
- **Unroll.Me:** Unsubscribe from unwanted emails to reduce digital clutter.
- **Google Photos:** Store and organize your digital photos.

Professional Services

- **Senior Move Managers:** Specialists who help with decluttering, packing, and moving.
- **Estate Sale Companies:** Professionals who can help you sell unwanted items.
- **Financial Planners:** Advisors who can help you navigate the financial aspects of downsizing.

FAQ: Common Downsizing Questions Answered

1. How do I decide what to keep and what to let go of?
Focus on items that are functional, meaningful, or bring you joy. Use the "keep, donate, discard" method and involve family members in the decision-making process.
2. What should I do with items I can't part with but don't have space for?
Consider digitizing photos and documents, or create a memory box for small keepsakes. For larger items, ask family members if they'd like them or explore storage options.
3. How can I make downsizing less overwhelming?
Break the process into smaller, manageable tasks. Focus on one room or category at a time, and don't hesitate to ask for help from family, friends, or professionals.
4. What if my family doesn't want my heirlooms?
Donate items to museums, historical societies, or charities. Alternatively, sell them through an estate sale or online marketplace.
5. How do I handle the emotional side of downsizing?

Acknowledge your feelings and give yourself permission to grieve. Focus on the positives, like the freedom and opportunities that come with a simpler lifestyle.

These appendices are designed to be your go-to resource as you navigate the downsizing process. Whether you're decluttering, planning a move, or managing finances, these tools will help you stay organized and confident every step of the way.

Good luck, and remember: this is your journey, and you've got this!

For Additional Support:
We are here to help. Request your free Social Security Analysis and retirement Income Plan. If you would like personalized guidance in maximizing your Social Security benefits and creating a comprehensive retirement income strategy, please contact:

Boom Retirement Solutions
(888) 839-1611

SCAN TO SCHEDULE

AN APPOINTMENT

For a free copy of our other book "Maximizing Social Security Benefits" send an email to jeff@boomretirement.com and in the Subject Line write "Free Book Social Security."

Made in the USA
Monee, IL
04 November 2026

67385769R00108